YOUR YOUTH

Getting the Best out of It

A person's youth can be one of the happiest periods of life. Unfortunately, for many it is not. Changing standards have created a mixed-up world, and today's problems often rob young people of happiness. This book is published to help them to see the solutions to these problems and so get the best out of life now and in the future.

—The Publishers

CONTENTS

The scriptures referred to in this book may be found in any translation of the Bible. However, unless otherwise indicated, direct quotations are from the modern-language *New World Translation of the Holy Scriptures*, 1971 edition.

CHAPTER 1

Living for Today and Tomorrow

YOUR youth should be a wonderful time of life. It is something like the spring season of the year. Youth is a time of fresh vitality. Your body is getting stronger and your mind is also developing. Many opportunities are opening up to learn and to do things. So there are lots of reasons why youth should be a happy and exciting time.

2 But is it, or will it be, for you? There are many things that can help or hinder in this. Some of these are things you can't do anything about. But many of them you can. This book is written in the hope that it will help you to get the best out of your youth, with long-lasting benefits.

3 Youth is a time of challenge. As you probably realize, the road of life today has plenty of rough spots. It takes courage to face them. But if you learn early how to overcome the rough spots, then the rest of the road becomes far smoother for you. Each time you win out over a problem your confidence will grow.

4 How much better it is to face the challenge of youth than to let the rough spots, the pressures and problems, sidetrack you. Of course, it would be easy just to dream or to kid yourself that life

1-5. Why should youth be a happy time? Yet what makes it challenging?

is different from what it really is. But sooner or later those who do that are sure to run into hard reality. It could then be very difficult to recover and move ahead. Valuable time would be lost because, as the saying goes, you are young only once.

⁵ Right now you are in a transition time, a period of change. Your body, for example, is moving toward physical maturity. But it doesn't reach that stage until sometime between the ages of twenty and twenty-three. It can take still longer for you to reach emotional maturity. Some of the changes taking place in you could make you feel confused or unsure of yourself. When you feel new pressures building up inside, how do you handle them? This book considers these changes that take place during youth and how to cope with them successfully. You can even enjoy meeting the challenges they bring, for they are all part of the remarkable experience of becoming an individual, a distinct person—*You*.

AIDS FOR CHARTING YOUR COURSE

⁶ Sometimes it may seem that your life is very restricted, filled with "do's" and "don'ts." But, thinking of it another way, when you're young you have a kind of freedom you won't have later on. Instead of being loaded down with all the responsibilities that older people have, you're free to spend a lot of time getting knowledge and developing your abilities and skills. You have much more time to learn about and to think about what other people have done or are doing. You can learn about their successes and their

6-9. How can you benefit by learning about what other people have done?

failures, and can see where they made wise choices or foolish mistakes. This can help you to know what direction you want to take on the road of life.

[7] Can you decide on that direction all on your own, without any help? How much sense would it make to try? Take some examples:

[8] Let's say you want to build a car engine. Would you start out to do it by yourself without first learning what experienced mechanics can tell you? If you did, how would the motor probably turn out? Or would you try to make a dress for a party without ever having seen anyone sew, or without a pattern? You can imagine what the dress would look like.

[9] Doesn't it almost go without saying that human living is a lot more complicated than a car engine or a party dress?

KEEP YOUR COMMUNICATION LINES OPEN

[10] It's a simple fact of life that every one of us builds on what others before us learned. But you can't do that without *communication*. With no communication—no talking, no reading, no observing of others so as to learn—there is no drawing on the knowledge and experience that others have gained.

[11] To get the best out of your youth you need to benefit from what others have learned. This includes such things as how to take the best care of your body, how to get and to keep really good friends, helpful guidelines as to dating and courting, and the answers to questions about marriage,

10-16. (a) Why do some youths feel that they don't want to learn from older people? How do you feel about that? (b) Besides listening to older persons, why do we also need some other source of information about life?

sex and the use of alcoholic drinks or drugs. These are all considered in this book.

[12] But maybe you are thinking about what you see today in the world around you. There is a lot of selfishness. Many people are being treated unfairly. There is also much cheating, pollution, crime, war, lying and hypocrisy. 'So what can I learn from older persons when they have made such a mess of things?' you may ask.

[13] True, many older persons today do bear guilt for these conditions. They either take part in the wrongs done or at least go along with and support the systems that produce those conditions.

[14] On the other hand, aren't there a lot of older persons who are just as disgusted at seeing the way things are going as you are? After all, these problems didn't just start to develop within one generation. When your parents were of the same age as you are now, they also found the world scene discouraging. In fact, for the past half century, particularly since the first world war of 1914-1918, people seem to be going from one crisis to another, each one getting harder to handle.

[15] Just being older or having more experience obviously doesn't bring all the answers to life's problems. Otherwise things everywhere would always be getting better. But they are not. So, then, in addition to the experience of others, is there another and even better source of information and help that you can tap?

[16] Yes, there is. We'll talk about that now.

CHAPTER 2

Why You Can
Look to the Future
with Confidence

HAVE you ever tried jumping over a bar in a high jump, or even over a fence or a wall? If the height was not too great, and you were confident that you could do it, you probably made the jump successfully. But if you were afraid you couldn't make it, the jump may have failed, with unpleasant consequences for you.

² That is the way it is with so many things. If you're afraid to go into the water, for example, you'll never learn to swim.

³ So, too, with getting the best out of your youth. Confidence can have a lot to do with this. You can't really be happy or make good progress on the road of life without confidence in what lies ahead. But today, what is there to merit our confidence?

⁴ We could spend a lot of time talking about the reasons for not having confidence. Our planet Earth is getting more and more polluted, its wildlife is being killed off, and there are food shortages and other serious problems. These things may make you wonder if there is anything worth looking forward to. Some young people feel that, with the way things on earth

---

1-4. What does confidence have to do with whether a person will succeed or not? Why is it that a lot of people don't feel very confident about the future?

are being ruined, there isn't much of a future for them. And it may indeed appear so. Yet there are a lot of things that people don't talk about so much but that give us reason to look forward to the future with confidence. Consider a few of these.

YOUR PLANETARY HOME

[5] It's easy for us to take the earth for granted. Yet this planet we were born on and live on is truly an amazing piece of work. Like a spinning ball, the earth travels through millions of miles of space as it circles the sun, 93 million miles (about 150,000,000 kilometers) away. What would happen if the earth were in a different position? Well, if it were as far away from the sun as, say, the planets Pluto and Neptune, the earth would be like a big deep-freeze, far too cold to live on. And if it were a third of the distance closer to the sun, as is the planet Venus, the earth would become like an oven, for the temperature would become so high that even lakes and rivers would boil.

[6] Or, even though its distance from the sun is ideal, what if the earth didn't rotate on its axis as it does every twenty-four hours? Suppose, like Mercury, it rotated only a little more than once during its annual trip around the sun. Then nearly one half of the earth would be a frozen sub-zero waste, with the remainder a deserted furnace.

[7] That isn't all. Why is it that, at least in much of the earth, we can enjoy the freshness and flowers of spring, the warm, sunny days of summer, the crispness and color of autumn and the beauty of winter snow? These seasons result from

5-8. Name some of the factors that make life possible on the earth. How did this amazing combination of things come about?

Knowledge about the Creator of the earth provides basis for confidence as to the future

the earth's being tilted at an angle relative to its path around the sun. The seasons help to make most of this planet's surface a very pleasant place to live. And they make it possible for a large part of the earth to produce food for man and animals.

⁸ There are hundreds of other factors that work together to make life on this planet possible. But what does all of this tell us? Ask yourself: How did this amazing combination of things come to be? Surely we must recognize that our planet Earth had a Designer. Yes, the many systems making life possible on earth are far, far more complicated than any spaceship that human scientists have designed and built. All the thought and work that earth's complicated systems represent also tell us something else. Clearly, they tell us that the Designer of the earth is interested in making life pleasant and happy for those who live here. That includes you.

⁹ True, a lot of people today are seriously damaging the earth by polluting it and misusing it. But that can be changed. And the damage can be reversed.

¹⁰ For example, consider what happened on the Pacific island of Krakatoa. It blew up in a huge volcanic explosion. If you had visited there right afterward, you would have seen that the whole island was just ashes. Nothing remained alive there—no people, no animals, no plants. But then what happened?

¹¹ Without anyone's help, the island began to recover. Within three years, some twenty-six kinds of plants began to flourish there again. Soon coconut trees, wild sugarcane and orchids

9-12. Even though a lot of damage has been done to the earth, what illustrates its ability to recover from harm?

were growing. And twenty-five years after the explosion, there were 263 species of animals on Krakatoa. The damage from the volcano disappeared. The gardenlike conditions of the island had returned.

[12] The amazing way the island of Krakatoa recovered can be repeated all over the earth. And, as we will see later in this book, there is good reason to believe that it will.

AN AMAZING FOOD FACTORY

[13] The next time you sit down to a meal, stop and think about this: No matter whether you are eating white rice or white potatoes, brown wheat or brown beans, yellow corn or yellow squash, black or red berries, they all come from plants with *green* leaves. Why? Because of the amazing process called photosynthesis.*

[14] Such plants all have a green substance in their leaves called chlorophyll. When the sun's light hits the leaves the chlorophyll goes to work producing complex chemical changes. In the plant's cells water and carbon dioxide (which the plant takes from the air) are combined to form a simple sugar, the basis of all food. Using that sugar, green plants also make more complex things like carbohydrates, fats, proteins and vitamins. Speaking of the astounding production that results from photosynthesis, botanist Frits W. Went says:

---

* From *photo,* meaning "light," and *synthesis,* meaning the "forming of a compound substance by combining simpler elements."

13-17. How is food produced from the earth? (Psalm 104:14) How does the *variety* of food that the earth produces contribute to one's enjoyment of life? So, what kind of life did the Designer of all these things have in mind for us? (Isaiah 25:6; Psalm 67:6)

"In terms of tonnage, its production makes man's industries seem trifling. Every year the world's steel mills turn out 350 million tons of steel, the world's cement factories 325 million tons of cement. The world's green plants, however, produce 150 *billion* tons of sugar every year.

15 Scientists know what happens, but they still can't understand just how photosynthesis works. As one science writer says, researchers often refer to the process as "the black box." Why? Because "they know what goes in and what comes out but are not sure about everything that goes on inside." With all their chemical laboratories, men can never duplicate this amazing process.

16 Almost as remarkable is the tremendous *variety of food* the earth produces. Perhaps you especially like some certain food—let's say strawberries. But what if everything—potatoes, rice, bread, apples, oranges—tasted like strawberries? You would soon get tired of that taste, wouldn't you? Instead, with the different fruits, vegetables, grains, nuts and berries that the earth's food factory produces, there are thousands of different flavors for your taste buds to enjoy.

17 Again, what does all of this tell us? Very obviously, the One who originated this amazing food factory wants life on this earth to be very pleasurable. He is concerned about a happy future for us. The same Designer that made planet Earth such an ideal home has also seen to it that this home is stocked with everything needed for a splendid banquet for those living here. Later on in this book we will also see just how He proposes to make that banquet available to all who want to share in it.

LOOK AT YOURSELF!

[18] Finally, think a little about yourself. To think, of course, you have to use your brain—so why not start there? Naturally, you can't see your brain, but what do you think it is like? When fully developed, the human brain looks like an oversized pinkish-gray walnut and weighs less than three pounds (1.3 kilos). But what tremendous ability is packed into that small area! A scientific report in the New York *Times* says:

> "The constitution of the brain . . . is so complex that it makes the giant electronic computers mere child's toys by comparison."

[19] Yes, the brain you possess and can use has been described as "the most complex piece of matter in the universe." Now, if someone gave you a fine watch or an expensive camera or a valuable electronic calculator, you would certainly care for it and try to get the best use out of it, right? You should feel far more appreciation for your brain.

[20] Think, too, of your body. Now, it's true that a lion is stronger than you are, an elephant is certainly bigger, a dolphin can swim faster, a monkey can climb better, an eagle can soar in the heights with its own wings and you can't. But none of these creatures combines in itself all the abilities that a man has. Lions and elephants can't fly, dolphins can't climb trees or mountains, nor can eagles swim. But humans can do all of these, either unaided or with their inventions. Yes, above all, humans are unique in their ability to make things, in endless variety.

[21] One reason for this is your hands. No tool

18-23. What is there about our bodies that shows that we were meant to be far superior to the animals?

ever invented can do all the things you can with your hands—from heavy work in mechanics or carpentry, to activities that call for a delicate touch, as in playing an instrument, painting or drawing the design for a house.

²² Really, your hands are just one of the things that make your body so marvelous. No wonder that Dr. W. W. Akers, an engineer working with surgeons, said of the human body:

> "The body is the ultimate in technological perfection. Almost any machine you can dream up—no matter how sophisticated—you can look into the body and find a better one."

²³ Clearly a Master Designer wanted humans to be far superior to the animals and to be able to enjoy the earth in the greatest way possible. This gives us reason to be confident that He is concerned about our enjoying a rewarding future.

YOU CAN MOVE AHEAD WITH CONFIDENCE

²⁴ We have seen that this planet and everything in it gives evidence of intelligence and design far superior to what is manifest in any home or building we have ever seen. You undoubtedly can agree with this simple statement found in the Bible: "Of course, every house is constructed by someone." (Hebrews 3:4) Suppose you went out into a vast desert and found a house there but didn't see anyone around. You wouldn't think that the house made itself, would you? So, too, the earth obviously has a Designer and Maker,

---

24-28. Why is it reasonable to believe that the earth had a Designer and Maker? (Romans 1:20) Where has he provided answers to our questions about life? (2 Timothy 3:16) How can we find out whether doing what the Bible says would really help us to face the future with confidence? (2 Peter 3:13; Revelation 21:1-4)

though unseen to us. Nobel Prize winner Max Planck said:

> "There is no explanation of the universe apart from the assumption of a Supreme Creative Intelligence."

²⁵ The Bible tells us who this "Supreme Creative Intelligence" is that constructed our home, the earth. It tells us that he is the Maker of heaven and earth, Jehovah God.

²⁶ This great Designer is obviously very powerful and wise. And just as clearly he has the best interests of all of us—you included—at heart. If you can learn what other humans know, then you can learn much, much more from Him as to how to get the best out of your youth.

²⁷ That is where the Bible comes in. It tells of the Creator's purposes for the earth and all mankind. It gives his answer to many questions humans have. It shows where their problems come from and how they will be solved. The Bible does not direct your hopes toward the present failing systems that have filled the earth with so much trouble and danger. It points to new systems that offer something far better.

²⁸ Whether you have read the Bible to some extent or not, you may wonder if what it says can really solve your problems and answer your questions. You will never know unless you look carefully into it. In this book that you are now reading, we will see what the Bible has to say and the answers and guidance it gives. See for yourself how reasonable and realistic the Bible is. Yes, see for yourself how Jehovah God's Word, the Bible, can help you to meet the challenge before you, and then move confidently ahead toward a happy and worthwhile future.

CHAPTER 3

Growing into Manhood

W E CAN benefit by looking at how we each
had our beginning as individuals. Just think
about it: Not so many years ago you were a
single fertilized egg cell smaller than the period
at the end of this sentence. From that tiny beginning, you began growing within your mother's
womb. In time your body was complete with a
brain that thinks, eyes that see, ears that hear,
and many other marvelous organs. How did this
remarkable growth take place?

² Your parents didn't draw up blueprints to
produce you. Rather, this was all done within
the fertilized egg that was formed by the uniting
of a sperm cell from your father with the egg cell
in your mother's womb. In a matter of minutes,
the plans were drawn up inside that tiny cell for
the entire new human that turned out to be you!

³ All the information needed to create you is
found in the DNA* of that tiny fertilized cell.
DNA is the essential substance of the tens of
thousands of genes in each cell, and these genes
are linked into twenty-three sets of chromosomes.
So much information is packed into each cell
that, if it were to be written out in human language, a whole roomful of books would be required. But perhaps even more amazing is the

---

* DNA is the code name for deoxyribonucleic acid.

1-6. What are some marvelous facts about our development up
till the time of birth? Is there anyone who deserves credit for
all of this? (Psalm 139:13-18)

fact that all this detailed information is passed along to each new cell of the body. So each cell has all the same information that the original fertilized egg contained!

⁴ But you may ask: How is the DNA able to use only the information it wants, and only when it wants to, for building a person's many different body parts? For instance, how does it manage to select only the instructions needed to build an eye? And when it builds an eye, how does it suppress all the information for building your ears, kidneys, liver, and so forth?

⁵ It is a mystery. Humans haven't figured it out. It is the design of a grand Creator! Because of what one of the writers of the Bible knew about the human body, he said to God: "I shall laud you because in a fear-inspiring way I am wonderfully made. Your works are wonderful, as my soul is very well aware." (Psalm 139: 14) Is that how you feel?

⁶ In only nine months the single fertilized cell with which you began became a fully developed baby, an amazingly complex organization of some billions of cells. Your growth will never again be so rapid! But about thirteen or fourteen years after your

In only nine months a single cell becomes a baby

birth, you begin another rapid spurt of growth. At this particular time you start changing from a boy into a man.* The entire transitional period, which is known as adolescence, lasts for a number of years. It ends when you reach physical maturity, generally between the ages of twenty and twenty-three. This period is not the easiest in your life, but it is very, very important. It is a proving ground for your future development.

CHANGES DURING PUBERTY

⁷ Puberty covers the earlier period of adolescence. Strictly, it is the age at which symptoms of sexual maturing appear. This age is commonly fixed at fourteen for boys and twelve for girls, but there is a wide variation in what is normal. You may have entered puberty at eleven or twelve, or you may be fifteen or sixteen and still not have begun maturing sexually. But an early or late maturing is not unusual, so there is no reason for concern. What are some of the problems you can expect during puberty?

⁸ For one thing, you may experience a certain awkwardness and lack of coordination. This is because your bones are lengthening and the muscles have to stretch along with them. In this expansion some parts of the body seem to grow rapidly, while others may lag. However, any resulting clumsiness will pass. It is no cause for great concern, though extra care is certain-

---

* The following chapter discusses the change from girlhood to womanhood.

7-12. (a) What changes occur in a male during puberty? Is there any reason to worry about these changes? (b) How can a young man tell when his sex organs have developed so that he can father children?

ly worth while, as it could save you from possible harm through some accident.

⁹ Among the body parts that are stretching out are the vocal cords. The extra length makes the voice deepen. But during the lengthening process your voice may often "crack," suddenly hitting a high note when you least expect it. Again, this is part of the "growing pains" of adolescence. So, when it happens and others are amused, just smile along with them and any embarrassment will quickly pass.

¹⁰ At the root of these body changes are your glands, including the thyroid, the adrenals and the gonads (sex glands). They produce yet other changes. One of them is the growth of hair around the organs of procreation, also under your armpits and on your chest. The amount varies from person to person and is no indicator whatsoever of how "manly" you are. Hair also begins to appear on the face. Though as yet this may be but a mere "fuzz," your encounter with the experience of shaving is steadily drawing near.

¹¹ Perhaps the change that most often is a source of disturbance for boys growing toward manhood involves the organs of procreation, the genitals. During puberty these not only attain their full size but also begin to function. The Bible, at Leviticus 15:16, 17, refers to 'emissions

of semen.' If your parents have failed to discuss the matter with you beforehand, your first emission of semen may be somewhat of an upsetting experience. What causes such emission?

[12] When you become developed enough to father children, then your sex organ begins to secrete the fluid called semen. It's a heavier fluid than water and, although there is not much of it, it contains millions of tiny sperm cells. Any one of these cells can fertilize a woman's egg cell and make it grow into a baby. More or less periodically your body will relieve itself of this semen. The emission usually takes place while you sleep and are dreaming.

PURPOSE OF SEX

[13] Our Creator provided sex as a means for a man to express deep love for a woman and to father their children. But God laid down rules regarding sex, explaining that sex relations are to be had only by a man and a woman who are married to each other. This is because God purposed that every baby brought into the world should have both a father and a mother who would take all the responsibility of rearing that child. It is, therefore, wrong in God's sight for persons who are not married to engage in sexual relations.

[14] On the other hand, for married persons sexual relations are a wonderful way for them to express love for each other. The husband lies close to his wife so that his male organ fits naturally into her birth canal. This can give great pleasure to each

---

13-15. (a) For what purpose did God provide sex? Why did he lay down rules to regulate it? (Hebrews 13:4) (b) Most likely, where is the best place to get reliable information about sex? (Proverbs 6:20)

of them. In the process, the husband's sperm cells go out of his body through his male organ right into his wife's birth canal. These sex cells move through the canal, and if a mature egg cell is there in the wife, one of her husband's sperm cells may join with it, and the fertilized cell will begin to grow into a baby. So you see, God made the sex organs for a sacred purpose, that of passing on life. That is why it is proper that they be used according to God's rules.

¹⁵ The best way to get answers to your questions about sexual development is to ask your parents, particularly your father. Your father has already experienced everything you have gone through and lots more. Also, whereas other youths might give you information that is only half right—a few facts and a lot of wild stories—your father should be able to give you good information that will help you and work for your happiness. If your father is not in a position to give you information or counsel based on God's Word, it would be valuable for you to know what God's Word says. You will find that elders in a congregation of Jehovah's Witnesses will be glad to be of help to you.

PROVING YOURSELF RESPONSIBLE

¹⁶ As you approach manhood it is natural for you to feel a desire for self-identity—to feel that you are a distinct person. It is also natural that you have a desire for a measure of independence. Your parents will likely begin preparing you for the time when you can be independent. How?

16-18. (a) In what ways have your parents encouraged you to exercise a measure of independence? How might what you do with those privileges affect your future opportunities? (b) Why do many young fellows join "gangs"? What might this lead to? (1 Corinthians 15:33)

¹⁷ No doubt by gradually giving you more responsibility and the privilege of sharing in making certain decisions as to things you will do. They may invite you to express your preference as to certain subjects you will take at school or they may let you take a part-time job. You may be allowed to do your own buying of some of your personal items. But whatever your parents see fit to do in this regard, it will then be up to you to show that you merit responsibility. If you act in a childish way or get "bigheaded," then they may have to reduce your privileges until you show yourself more of a man.

¹⁸ This desire for greater self-identity and a measure of independence is accompanied by other natural desires. You will feel a need to be appreciated by others for what you are and what you can do. Some youths seek to satisfy their desire for self-identity and 'a sense of belonging' by joining or forming "gangs." But such gangs generally make their own code of conduct, and the facts show that this almost always leads to wrongdoing, at times even to serious crimes. Probably more than any other single factor, bad companionship is to be found at the root of the problem when young men get into trouble.

¹⁹ During this period of life you begin to get some idea of what you are going to look like physically as a grown man. But you should also start thinking more and more about what you are going to be like inside, what the Bible calls "the secret person of the heart." (1 Peter 3:4) This stage of your life is not the time to let a desire for increased independence somehow divide

---

19, 20. Why is a good relationship with your parents important? What could damage it? (Proverbs 23:24, 25)

you off from your parents and the rest of the family. The changes you are experiencing during puberty, and the new urges you feel and have to learn to control, actually increase your need for their love and steadying influence.

[20] So instead of drawing away from your parents and letting a gap develop, draw closer to them and learn all that you can from them as you now approach adulthood. You will never regret this. And you will bring them real happiness too, making them proud to have you as their son.

CHAPTER 4

Moving into Womanhood

SPRINGTIME eventually passes into summer. Flowering trees in time become fruit-bearing trees. So, also, do young girls naturally become young women. As when a bud has opened up, revealing what the flower is like, so, too, when this transitional period of adolescence is over, the woman you are going to become is more clearly evident. In this development there is much you can do to contribute toward happy results.

[2] During your adolescent years, you grow taller, adding perhaps five or six inches (12 to 15 centimeters) to your height. You also become heavier. As a rule, there will be a couple of years when you experience a "growth spurt," a time when your rate of growth in height and weight

---

1-3. During adolescence, what might cause a girl concern as to her own physical growth? But what eventually happens?

speeds up remarkably. You may see other girls of your same age suddenly outgrowing you, or you may find yourself swiftly outgrowing them. Either way, there is no need to become concerned about this. Each individual's time for this rapid growth period comes at its own point. Girls generally enter this "growth spurt" a year or two earlier than boys. There is, in fact, a time when girls may tend to be taller than boys of the same age. But the boys catch up and, since their growth continues longer than that of girls, generally the boys finish up taller and stronger.

³ Sometimes this growth spurt is initially more rapid in one part of the body than in another. Your feet or hands may seem to become distressingly long in proportion to the rest of your body. But, in time, the rest of the body gets into the swing of growth and things equalize. Usually the lengthening of the torso and the deepening of the chest cavity develop last. Facial contours change. At the same time other parts of the body begin to develop fatty deposits that give the rounded form of the feminine figure.

OTHER BODILY CHANGES

⁴ But another development takes place during feminine adolescence. It is the start of what Rachel, a woman spoken of in the Bible, called "the customary thing with women," menstruation. (Genesis 31:34, 35) In a sense, it is a thrilling moment—it shows that you have reached the threshold of womanhood. Hormone secretions have

---

4-6. (a) What "customary thing with women" begins during adolescence? What purpose is served by this bodily process? (b) What other physical changes also occur at this time, and why?

begun to work in your body. They stimulate your ovaries to begin releasing egg cells, quite irregularly at first, but then about once every four weeks. The egg cell, when released, passes down into your womb, which has been stimulated to develop a special lining for receiving the egg in case it should become fertilized. When the egg remains infertile, this lining is in time discarded. This is what produces menstruation, the periodic discharge of blood, fluid and some tissue. While some accompanying pain or discomfort may be experienced, it is a normal process and should cause no undue concern.

[5] When do these monthly cycles begin? Their start varies from person to person. While in many lands the average is at around thirteen years, one girl may begin menstruating as early as ten years of age or even earlier, while another may not begin until sixteen or even later. Similarly, the length of the menstrual flow may vary from three to five days.

[6] Along with this change from childhood to womanhood, there is a broadening of your hips, and your breasts begin to develop. These many developments, some visible, some invisible, are all preparations for the dual role in life that mankind's Creator has reserved for women—that of being a wife and a mother. The broader hips that girls develop not only aid in making childbirth easier but also make it easier to carry small children. During pregnancy the normal fatty deposits on the woman's body are a reserve supply that can be drawn on as she nourishes unborn or newly born children, and with birth the breasts begin producing milk.

GROWING ATTRACTION TO MEN

⁷ The privileges granted to women by mankind's Creator, Jehovah God, carry with them the responsibility to respect and act in harmony with the Creator's purpose. The mutual attraction that God has caused to exist between the sexes is largely related to procreation. As a girl's body develops so that she is capable of bearing children, she exerts a stronger attraction toward males who have reached the stage of being able to father children. But this attraction can be misused or abused. What, then, needs to be kept in mind so that you

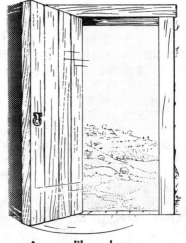

Are you like a door . . .

can take the right course, one that will contribute to your lasting future happiness and assure God's blessing?

⁸ In the Bible book The Song of Solomon we find an interesting expression evidently made by the older brothers of a maiden from Shulem. First, one is quoted as saying: "We have a little sister that does not have any breasts. What shall we do for our sister on the day that she will be

---

7-10. (a) How does the development of a girl's body place upon her added responsibility as to her conduct? (b) How is this responsibility illustrated in The Song of Solomon by the comparisons of a certain girl to "a wall" and "a door"?

spoken for?" That is, what would they do for their sister when she had ceased to be flat-chested, had grown up and someone now asked to arrange for her marriage? Another brother answered, saying: "If she should be a wall, we shall build upon her a battlement of silver; but if she should be a door, we shall block her up with a cedar plank." (Song of Solomon 8:8, 9) What does this mean?

⁹ Their figurative language apparently meant that if their sister proved to be firm as a "wall" they would handsomely reward and honor her. How could she prove firm as a wall? By showing firm determination to remain chaste, showing strength in resisting any attempts to involve her in immoral conduct. When suitable for marriage, she would show herself steady and constant in holding to right principles. On the other hand, if she was like a "door" that swings open to anyone exerting a little strength toward it, even to someone unwholesome, then they would have to take steps to restrict her, in effect, to 'bar her shut' as someone not to be trusted as regards the opposite sex. She could also be like a door that swings open and shut in her affections, becom-

. . . or like a wall?

ing infatuated first with one person and then rejecting him for another.

[10] The Shulammite maiden, now a matured woman with breasts, successfully passed this test and was able to say to her brothers: "I am a wall, and my breasts are like towers. In this case I have become in his eyes [that is, the eyes of her prospective husband] like her that is finding peace."—Song of Solomon 8:10.

[11] You, too, face a similar test as you approach womanhood. If you want to enjoy true peace of mind, heart and conscience, and protect yourself against experiencing peace-wrecking problems, you need to exercise self-control and show strength for what is right. Ought you to draw attention deliberately to those parts of your body that relate to motherhood by wearing short, snug-fitting skirts, low-cut blouses or tight sweaters? That would have a sexually stimulating effect on those of the opposite sex. Then what?

[12] Well, will you have the firmness and strength to resist all advances that such emphasis on those body parts might induce? And, even though you show physical development, do you have the mental and emotional development you would need for marriage and possible motherhood? A cat is ready to have kittens at twelve months of age and instinctively can do a good job of caring for her offspring. But humans are not creatures of instinct like animals. Humans have to learn far more than they inherit, and learning takes time. To try to rush the process would be like trying to force the petals of a rosebud to open

---

11-14. (a) Why might the wearing of short skirts or tight sweaters lead to unwanted problems for a young woman? (b) As a young woman, for what reasons especially would you like to be attractive to a young man?

before their time. That would only ruin the flower and damage any future beauty it might have. Remember, too, marriage is not just being a bride. It also means being a housekeeper, a cook and a clothes washer, and being a mother requires great patience and endurance toward children—all of this in good times and bad, in sickness and in health.

[13] Besides this, even though a young woman might feel that she is prepared for marriage, what kind of husband does she want to try to attract? If a young man is attracted simply by what a girl appears to be able to give in the way of sexual satisfaction, is he likely to make a good husband? Rather than trying to attract on that basis, would it not be far better to seek enduring friendships on the basis of what you are as a person—in your mind and heart? You can do that by developing personality traits that are attractive to others. Also, by such things as your conversation, by showing a wholesome, cheerful outlook on life, by showing that you appreciate such things as honesty, modesty, decency, kindness and unselfishness.

[14] You can prove that you are genuine in this by refusing to throw away these fine qualities for a few moments of pleasure that would only cheapen and lower you in your own estimation and in that of others whom you respect, admire and cherish. Especially by showing that you have truly worthwhile goals in life, that you want to 'remember your Creator in the days of your young womanhood,' can you gain as friends persons whose friendship you will always treasure and which can bring you real happiness.—Ecclesiastes 12:1.

PROPER VIEW OF APPEARANCE

[15] It is natural for teen-age girls to be concerned with their personal appearance. But do not be overly anxious or dissatisfied with your physical form or face, as if your whole future depended on this. Look at the grown-ups around you—people you like and admire. Are not many, perhaps most of them, of rather ordinary appearance? Physical attractiveness is not the real key to future happiness.

[16] And this is just as true of the girl who does have physical beauty. She should realize that

---

15, 16. (a) Though it's natural to be concerned about your physical appearance, what will have a far greater effect on your future happiness? (b) In terms of everyday life, explain Proverbs 11:22. Also Proverbs 31:30.

Do you put too great an emphasis on physical appearance?

many beautiful women wind up leading very empty, and often immoral, lives. How true is the Bible proverb: "As a gold nose ring in the snout of a pig, so is a woman that is pretty but that is turning away from sensibleness"! (Proverbs 11: 22) Yes, as the Bible also says, "charm may be false, and prettiness may be vain; but the woman that fears Jehovah is the one that procures praise for herself."—Proverbs 31:30.

STRIVING FOR EMOTIONAL BALANCE

[17] The physical changes of adolescence may bring emotional changes. Even as a young girl may feel full of energy one minute and exhausted the next, so too her emotions may tend to fluctuate widely. Periods of brightness and joy may be quickly followed by periods of gloom and depression. You may find yourself wondering if you are really normal or just what kind of person you are turning out to be. Especially in the modern industrial society, with its shifting sets of values, adolescent girls are subject to tension and uncertainty.

[18] It would be easy to give in to this instability, become withdrawn, introverted, or become very independent and assertive. Some girls do give in to displays of rudeness, flashes of bad temper or coarse speech. Others begin to make a pretense of being something they are not, becoming superficial. But this does not help; it only worsens matters. Now that you are coming out of childhood, it is a time to make a serious personal

---

17-19. (a) What emotional changes may a girl experience during adolescence? What can help her to attain emotional balance? (Galatians 5:22, 23) (b) What personal habits can also contribute to one's stability?

effort to cultivate the fruits of God's spirit—love, joy, peace, long-suffering, kindness, goodness, faith, mildness and self-control.

[19] Cultivate, too, habits that contribute toward stability. Instead of letting your room become messy, keep it orderly and neat. Strive for regularity in sleeping and eating habits; your developing body needs all the help you can give it. The more you can do along these lines, the more calm and stable you will feel, and this will help to moderate your emotional experiences.

[20] By all means do not let this period of transition cause you to pull away from your parents. They can provide the solid help and reliable firmness you need to lean on so as to keep your balance during this time of change. While you are subject to much "peer pressure"—pressure from others of your age to be like them—realize that they themselves are changing. That is why what pleases them today may not please them at all tomorrow. To be overly concerned about what they think of you will only increase your problems. That is why, too, when you have personal, intimate questions, your parents are by far the better source of information. They can give you a much fuller, more balanced answer than your schoolmates could ever give.

[21] Just as early showers are followed by pretty flowers, so, too, if you learn to weather the storm and take things in your stride, you will find the way to stability and confidence. While you should be concerned about keeping yourself

20, 21. (a) When you have questions about life, why will you get more reliable information from your parents than from other teen-agers? (b) What, in particular, will make you a truly attractive person?

physically well and clean (by good diet and regular hygiene), you need to concentrate—not so much on what you are on the outside—but on what you are on the inside. The adornment of a "quiet and mild spirit" produced by the 'secret person of your heart' is what will make you truly attractive—in the eyes of God and of humans.—1 Peter 3:3, 4.

CHAPTER 5

Masturbation and Homosexuality

ISN'T it remarkable how the bodies of boys and girls develop during adolescence so that they can either father children or give birth to them? Along with this physical transformation of your body, there is usually a change in your attitude toward the opposite sex. An attraction grows, and often boys develop a keen interest in girls, and girls in boys. But, at the same time, you may have a certain wonderment and curiosity about your own rapidly changing body. How should you satisfy this curiosity? Should you experiment with your sex organs? Is there anything wrong with rubbing them in some way until the excitement is climaxed?

[2] This practice is called masturbation. It is very common. One authority on the subject says:

1-4. (a) What is masturbation? (b) Why does the fact that a practice is common not necessarily make it right? (c) Why should we be interested in God's view on this matter?

"Every serious statistical study that we have shows clearly that . . . at least ninety-five per cent of boys and young men between thirteen and twenty-five years of age pass through periods of habitual masturbation of varying lengths." As for girls, this source says that "forty to fifty per cent are found to actually masturbate." Some people say that these figures prove "normalcy" and that the "absence of masturbation in a healthy youth is a matter of concern."

[3] Now, what do you think? Do you agree that, because in today's world masturbation is a very common thing, this makes it a natural, normal function of the body? Lying and stealing are also common today. Yet you wouldn't say this makes them natural and proper, would you? The "common" cold is quite universal, but this certainly doesn't mean that you want it, does it? Then what about the claim that masturbation is harmless?

[4] From a physical standpoint, the majority of doctors say that occasional masturbation is harmless. Like most psychiatrists, they say that damage comes only if the practicer has feelings of guilt that cause mental and emotional disturbance, these, in turn, producing physical upset. But doctors and psychiatrists are imperfect humans, subject to error, and their views change. There is, though, a source of counsel that young people can turn to that is stable and free from error or misjudgment. That is God's Word. And if we want, not just longer life, but everlasting life in God's favor, we should seek his wisdom and counsel. He can do for us and for our happiness what men could never do.

VIEW OF A HIGHER SOURCE

[5] The real question, then, is, not how much physical harm could result from masturbation, but whether spiritual harm results. True, the words "masturbation" and "self-abuse" do not appear in the Bible. But what do you understand from the inspired counsel of the apostle Paul at Colossians 3:5? To those not wanting to lose God's approval, he says: "Deaden [Do not *excite*], therefore, your body members that are upon the earth as respects fornication, uncleanness, sexual appetite, hurtful desire, and covetousness." Unlike fornication, masturbation is something a person may do by himself or herself. But does that keep it from being unclean? Or is it also a giving in to, and being dominated by, "sexual appetite"?

[6] Then, too, the apostle writes of those who "gave themselves over to loose conduct to work uncleanness of every sort with greediness." (Ephesians 4:19) In his letter to the Colossians, quoted in the previous paragraph, Paul mentioned "covetousness," and in this text, "greediness." Really, masturbation expresses both of these undesirable qualities. How? Well, it is an expression of desiring something that does not rightly belong to one. God has provided marriage as the arrangement in which to satisfy sexual desires. But the person who practices masturbation is, in effect, trying to obtain that satisfaction without paying the price. The price is the assuming and shouldering of the responsibilities that go along with marriage. In this connection note that, when the apostle counseled persons who were 'inflamed with passion,' he did

_____
5, 6. (a) How does the counsel at Colossians 3:5 relate to masturbation? (b) Why does the Bible associate this practice with "covetousness" and "greediness"?

not tell them to seek relief through masturbation, but through God's provision of marriage.—1 Corinthians 7:2, 9.

[7] Actually, masturbation may endanger your future happiness in marriage. If a person is used to satisfying his or her passions through masturbation, this develops the habit of thinking only of one's own pleasure and satisfaction. But in marriage there is need, especially on the part of the man, to show concern for the other person's pleasure and satisfaction as well. Otherwise, marital relations deteriorate and there is distress and disillusionment. This very situation—husbands thinking of their own satisfaction and disregarding their wives' needs—is one of the greatest problems in marriage. Much of it stems from a premarital masturbation habit.

[8] "But," some persons might ask, "what if one is too young to make marriage advisable? While postponing marriage, would not masturbation protect one against some worse violation of God's law, such as fornication or homosexuality?" It might seem so. But is that sound reasoning? No. Masturbation weakens a healthy conscience and love for what is right, the very things that can protect one against such practices. Like drug addiction, masturbation can become something that one resorts to every time he or she feels tension of any kind and lacks the will to face up to and overcome the problems causing such tension. So it can produce a vicious cycle, eventually making a person its slave. But God says we should control our bodies, not let them control us.

7, 8. (a) If masturbation becomes a habit, how can it affect one's prospects of a happy marriage? (b) Why would it be a mistake to view masturbation as a means to avoid serious violation of God's law?

HOMOSEXUAL PRACTICES

[9] Weakly giving in to sexual desires by masturbation will certainly not give you strength when faced with a situation tempting you to commit fornication—or even homosexuality. Just the opposite, it cultivates wrong thinking and wrong desire. In fact, masturbation can lead into homosexuality. In such instances the person, not satisfied with his lonely sexual activity, seeks a partner for mutual sex play.

[10] This happens much more frequently than you may realize. Contrary to what many persons think, homosexuals are not *born* that way, but their homosex-

> **Are homosexuals born that way, or is their behavior learned?**

ual behavior is learned. And often a person gets started when very young by playing with another's sexual parts, and then engaging in homosexual acts. One young man relates:

[11] "When I was young, I had very little parental guidance. I was allowed to go my own way, and do my 'own thing.' It was when I was only about eight years old that my older cousins introduced me to homosexual acts. I found these pleasurable, and so continued the practice with them and later with others. Soon it was almost a daily activity. At first I had no realization of doing

9-13. (a) How does masturbation sometimes make one vulnerable to homosexual practices? Is anyone born a homosexual? (b) How does God view such practices? (c) Is it possible to break free from them? (Romans 1:24-27; Leviticus 18:22, 23; 1 Corinthians 6:9-11)

anything wrong. My parents had not given me any instruction regarding moral conduct, and I never confided in them.

[12] "We then lived in a Central American country. Later we moved to New York city, where I finished high school. I also continued homosexual practices. The schools and city are filled with homosexuals, so there were plenty of opportunities. As I grew older I realized that what I was doing was unnatural, and was not right. But I continued because I wanted to. These sex acts had become very enticing to me."

[13] The youth was "hooked" on the practices, and it was only after great effort that he was able to overcome them. What motivated him to change? It was a desire to please Jehovah God. When he understood that God views homosexual acts as "unnatural," and that He totally disapproves of them, the young man fought these practices until he had conquered them. God's Word is very clear on this matter, saying: "Make no mistake: no fornicator or idolater, none who are guilty either of adultery or of homosexual perversion . . . will possess the kingdom of God." —1 Corinthians 6:9, 10, *The New English Bible*.

OVERCOMING WITH SELF-CONTROL

[14] What you think about has a lot to do with the way you feel and the things you do. So what do you really want? Do you want to feel disturbed by sexual desire most of the time, habitually masturbating, and perhaps even slipping into homosexual practices? This can happen if you let your

14-16. (a) What can be done to keep sexual desires subdued? (Philippians 4:8; 1 Thessalonians 4:3-5) (b) If you feel sexual passion building up, what can you do to get relief? (Psalm 1:1, 2; 63:6, 7)

mind dwell on sexual matters. But if you want to keep such sexual urge from cutting into your enjoyment of life and your really accomplishing worthwhile things, then exercise self-control and turn your mind to other matters.

[15] When pictures, reading matter or other things containing sexually stimulating material come your way, do not weakly give in. If you let your mind dwell on such things or engage in conversation that revolves around them, you will pay the consequences in feeling upset and in the building up of pressure within yourself. That is because the longer you look at or talk about such things

Does what you read matter?

the deeper your heart becomes involved. And your heart is a major factor in moving you to act.

[16] But what if, under even ordinary circumstances, you feel passion building up within you? How can you find relief? Not by resorting to masturbation, but by getting your mind, heart and body onto another track. You can do some work, engage in physical exercise, play a game or go for a walk. It is good to find someone to talk to who has your respect, even call someone like that on the phone if necessary. Reading— even aloud—the Bible or publications explaining the Bible is one of the finest helps. And, above

all, take the problem to your heavenly Father, Jehovah God, in prayer.

¹⁷ There are, of course, many additional things of a simple and sensible nature that one can do to help to avoid or reduce sexual tension. Being with others—provided, of course, that they are wholesome persons—is a protection. If you sleep in a room alone and you find that you seem to feel special stress in this direction at night, you may be able to arrange matters to share a room with another member of your family. Also, you may find it helpful to sleep on your side rather than on your back or face down.

¹⁸ Another thing that may be helpful is to see to it that your clothing does not unnecessarily cause friction with the sexual organs. Before retiring, try to see that what you read or talk about has a calming effect rather than the opposite. So, too, with any eating that you do at this time. Some have even found that if they limit the amount of food and drink they consume before retiring they sleep more soundly and are not so inclined to be aroused sexually. And especially important is good masculine or feminine hygiene. Lack of cleanliness can produce irritation of the genital organs and pull one's attention in that direction. You can inquire of your parents for information on such matters of personal hygiene.

¹⁹ Proper hygiene calls for certain handling of the sex organs, and one might feel that this would be a temptation to misuse them. But because your

---

17-20. (a) How might adjustments in one's habits in relation to sleep, eating and hygiene be helpful? (b) Even if a person is having a hard struggle to do what is right, why should he not feel that his situation is hopeless? (Psalm 103:13, 14)

motive is right—with the aim of *avoiding* sexual tension—you may well find that such care will instead help you to take a more healthful view toward these organs. You will appreciate that they were never meant to 'take you over' and rule your whole life.

[20] If you are now fighting the practice of masturbation, remember: You are certainly not the first or the only one who has faced this problem. Even though you find yourself having a hard struggle to break a masturbation habit, never feel that Jehovah God and his Son Jesus Christ have given up on you. If you sincerely keep working to overcome it, they will kindly and patiently help you to build up the needed strength so that you come off victorious.

CHAPTER 6

Caring for Yourself Physically

THE wise man Solomon likened the human body to a house with windows and doors. Centuries later, the Christian apostle Paul called it "this dwelling house." (Ecclesiastes 12:3-7; 2 Corinthians 5:1, 2) Like a house, your body needs proper care if you are to get full benefit from it.

2 What kind of housekeeper are you when it comes to caring for yourself physically? Do you appreciate the body you have? You should, for the human body is truly a masterpiece among all earth's creations. Your body is more complex than any computer or mechanical device ever invented. Yet it is smooth-working, wonderfully efficient and extremely flexible. It is staggering to think how all the bones, muscles, blood vessels, the network of nerve systems, plus all the other organs and parts of the human organism, function together harmoniously as one unit. As the apostle Paul wrote, though having many members, "the body is one." We do well to remember that and to realize also the truth of his statement that, "if one member suffers, all the other members suffer with it." Yes, despite its billions of cells, the body is a unit. If you want to get the best out of your youth and your whole life, you cannot afford to neglect any part of your body.—1 Corinthians 12:12, 14-26.

1, 2. In what ways is the human body a real masterpiece?

44

³ But there is a better, higher reason for wanting to give your body the best care you can. That is so you can use it to bring honor to your Creator, as well as to your parents, and to bring good to your neighbor. A house poorly cared for brings no credit to the architect or the builder. A house that is run-down, unclean or that gives off offensive odors adversely affects all the surrounding neighborhood. The same is true with us if we fail to care properly for ourselves physically.

⁴ The Bible principle that 'we reap what we sow' is true in our care of the body. (Galatians 6:7) The "harvest" can be good or bad, depending on us. And a person does not have to wait until he or she is aged to begin reaping. It starts much, much sooner, sometimes very early in life.

⁵ It is not just a matter of trying to avoid "getting sick." You should want to enjoy that feeling of well-being that contributes to happiness, to good work, to clear thinking, and that helps to make you an agreeable person to be around. What, then, are some of the things that merit regular attention?

THE VALUE OF A BALANCED DIET

⁶ The food you eat does much more than just provide energy. It provides the building materials your body needs to maintain itself. Carbohydrates, such as are found in sugar, bread and potatoes, give you energy. But what if your diet is almost entirely of such things? What if you were to try

3-5. (a) Who is affected by how you care for your body? (Romans 14:7, 8) (b) As regards care of the body, how is it true that 'we reap what we sow'?
6-8. Give some details on the value of a balanced diet as regards (a) carbohydrates, (b) proteins, (c) minerals, and (d) vitamins.

to get by on soft drinks and candy? Your body would begin to suffer from lack of the materials needed to make daily repairs.

7 You regularly need proteins, such as are found in milk, cheese, beans, meat and fish. Without them your muscles soon become soft and flabby, and growth is retarded. You need minerals, for without them your teeth will soon deteriorate and your bones will weaken. Leafy vegetables are rich in minerals. You need vitamins, because these are chemical regulators of the body and they protect the body against certain diseases. Fruits and cereals are major sources of vitamins. And you need plenty of water, for it forms the basis for your blood and all your tissue fluids.

8 Not just when you are sixty or seventy, but right in your teens you can reap the results of good diet or bad diet. Research has shown, for example, that when students were given an improved diet their learning capacity also improved. Poor diet generally re-

Eating a balanced diet is vital to good health

sults in poor work and makes people more accident-prone. It quickly robs the body of a healthy appearance and natural beauty.

CLEANLINESS CONTRIBUTES TO HEALTH

[9] Just as we get far more enjoyment out of living in a clean house, so, too, we get more enjoyment out of life if we keep our bodies clean. Regular bathing is refreshing and healthful. Your body comes in constant contact with microscopic germs, in the air and in the things you handle. Some of these can bring disease. Soap acts as a germicide to kill these, while water serves to wash them away. Your hands especially need frequent attention, for they handle your food and with them you may touch other persons or handle things they use.

[10] You not only feel better when you keep yourself clean; you also make life more pleasant for those who see you or come near you. If you see a house that is dirty and unkempt, what opinion do you form of the people living in it? So, too, people tend to judge you by your appearance. Dirt on your face, in your ears, on your neck, in your hair, on your hands or under your fingernails can hinder you in gaining others' friendship and esteem. Also, you will have more self-respect if you keep yourself clean.

[11] The body perspires, even when one does not do a lot of exercise or work. If perspiration accumulates, it can cause your body to have an unpleasant odor. Regular bathing, washing under the arms and similar places, helps to make you a more enjoyable person to be around. Cleanliness, along with good diet, also contributes toward a better, clearer complexion.

[12] The teeth are a particular area needing at-

9-14. (a) How can regular bathing protect your health? (b) How will your habits as to personal cleanliness affect the way others view you, and why? (c) Why is regular and careful cleaning of the teeth important? (d) What does the Bible itself say about cleanliness? (Exodus 30:17-21; Matthew 6:17, 18)

tention. Food particles may lodge between them or on them. The acids these particles give off attack the enamel of your teeth. After repeated attacks, sometimes within a matter of months, the hard enamel is penetrated and decay sets in. Or you may develop an inflammation of the gums that can, in time, cause the teeth to loosen. You may lose some of them. Decayed or missing teeth detract from your appearance.

[13] A clean mouth is also a safeguard against offensive breath. Drinking several glasses of water daily helps. Remember, your mouth is somewhat like the door or entrance of a house. If the appearance of the house and odors coming from the door are not good, people will tend to shy away.

[14] While not going to extremes (as some persons do in this matter), God's Word the Bible encourages and teaches cleanliness. Clean hands and freshly bathed bodies are often used to stand for one's being spiritually clean and pure. And the apostle Paul exhorted: "Let us cleanse ourselves of every defilement of flesh and spirit, perfecting holiness in God's fear." (2 Corinthians 7:1) Are we clean inside, in our hearts and minds? Then should we not strive to be clean outside as well?

NEED FOR PROPER REST

[15] During each day millions of the body's cells break down and need to be replaced. Your body builds up certain wastes that collect in the muscles, especially as the result of work and exercise. These wastes are what give you a tired feeling.

15-18. (a) Why does the human body need rest and sleep? (b) Even if you feel that you have energy to keep going, how will you be affected if you do not get enough rest? (c) How does our caring for ourselves physically show respect for God?

Your body must have sufficient rest if it is to rid itself of the accumulated wastes and also be able to produce new cells to keep your body in good shape and repair. Your central nervous system and your brain, too, need rest. These simply cannot relax unless you sleep.

¹⁶ Being young, you may feel that you can get along with little sleep. But youthful vigor and energy can be deceptive. They can mask the symptoms of serious damage that may be developing due to insufficient rest. Actually, a young

Your body needs sufficient rest to rid itself of wastes

person's growing body needs more sleep than that of an adult, not less. Lack of sleep impairs thinking and increases forgetfulness. It slows down one's alertness and the body's reflexes. It can make you tense, restless, irritable and hard to get along with. This is especially true under conditions of pressure and stress.

¹⁷ So, cooperate with your body by giving it the rest it needs. When your parents instruct you to be in bed at a certain hour, realize the rightness of their guidance. By your getting sufficient sleep each night, the quality and speed of your work will improve. You will find life more pleasant and will have fewer complaints.

¹⁸ If we appreciate the gift of life we enjoy in our bodies, then we should use them to the honor of our Maker and also to that of His Son, who gave his life that we might gain eternal life. We should never misuse or neglect our bodies due to mere carelessness or stupidity or for selfish reasons. This would show lack of respect for the One to whom we owe our lives. Rather, let us follow the Bible admonition: "Whether you are eating or drinking or doing anything else, do all things for God's glory." He will richly reward and bless you for the appreciation you show for his loving provisions.—1 Corinthians 10:31.

CHAPTER 7

Your Clothes and Appearance Talk —About YOU

HAVE you ever admired the pleasing varieties of color in a field of spring flowers or marveled at the beautiful shades to be found among tropical fish? Seeing these things convinces us that our Creator appreciates variety and beauty. He does not want everything to look dull, gray or monotonous. And how interesting it is to see the great variety of styles among people around the world! But have you stopped to think how

1-4. Why does the way we dress tell something about what we are like inside? Give examples.

much the way you look on the outside tells about what you're like on the inside?

² When you were very small your clothing probably didn't tell much about the kind of person you were. Your parents picked out your clothes for you and combed your hair. But as you grew older they allowed you to have more say about selecting your clothing, how you arranged your hair and such things. Now your own choice came into play. More and more your appearance came to reflect what you're like inside, your own personality. What do your clothes and appearance tell about you?

KEEPING YOUR BALANCE

³ People who are very proud of themselves often show it by being extremely style-conscious. They always want to "outshine" everybody else with their clothes or looks. But pride or selfishness can also be revealed by being very sloppy. Why? Because while the sloppy person may be just lazy, he may also have a selfish "don't care" attitude as to the effect his appearance has on others. Between these two extremes is the person who doesn't think too much of himself and who cares about others. His appearance will show it by good taste and moderation.

⁴ Some young persons feel they have to keep up with all the latest styles so as not to look old-fashioned. But in between being "ultra-conservative" and very "mod" there is a middle ground. If you stay with that, then you'll always be well-dressed and you won't be reacting to every single fashion change, like a puppet twitching each time a string is pulled.

⁵ Ask yourself: Who benefits anyway from my being very style-conscious? It's the commercial world that basically sets and encourages styles. They have one big interest: to make money. If you always play into their hands you'll benefit them, but you really won't benefit yourself in any genuine way.

⁶ Sloppiness may not seem to cost you much money but it can cost you a lot in other ways. It can cost you a job or cost you the respect of others. Even if a person's clothes aren't expensive, if he keeps them neat and clean, this shows he has self-respect. Oth-

5-7. (a) Who really benefits when a person tries to keep up with all the latest styles of clothing? (b) Even if a person does not have much money, how can his clothing show that he has self-respect? (c) How might the principles found at Philippians 2:3, 4 and Romans 15:2 be applied to how we dress?

er people respect him more and have more confidence in him.

⁷ A good rule to follow in all life's affairs is found in the Bible at Romans 15:2: "Let each of us please his neighbor in what is good for his upbuilding." Other people look at us more than we look at ourselves. So, then, shouldn't we try to give them something they will find pleasant to look at? Not something that makes them feel self-conscious because of their own appearance, but something that shows we care about their feelings.

IDENTIFIED BY DRESS

⁸ The way you dress tells something about you in another way. It can identify you with a certain group or class. This was true even thousands of years ago, when the Bible was being written.

What do your clothes say about you?

For example, in the book of Second Kings we read of messengers reporting back to King Ahaziah and telling of meeting a man who gave them a certain message. The king asked: "What was the appearance of the man?" When they described his garments, the king said immediately: "It was Elijah." How did he know? Because Elijah wore the distinctive garment of a prophet.—2 Kings 1:2, 5-8.

⁹ To be identified as a prophet was an honorable

8-11. (a) How are various groups or types of people identified by their dress? (b) So, what may people conclude from the way a person dresses, and how might this present problems?

thing. But another Bible example shows that one's dress could also link one up with that which is dishonorable. To attain a certain purpose, Judah's daughter-in-law Tamar took off garments identifying her as a widow and put on a shawl and a veil and sat alongside the road. When Judah came along, the record says that "he at once took her for a harlot, because she had covered her face [with the veil]." Her dress gave her the appearance of a prostitute of that time. —Genesis 38:13-15.

[10] Today, just as back then, the way we dress can link us up with certain classes of persons, even though we may not practice what they practice or believe what they believe. People assume that we at least sympathize with the class of persons who dress that way. Can we blame them?

[11] Manner of dress distinguishes not only policemen, firemen or nurses; it also distinguishes people whose occupation is dishonorable. Today prostitutes seldom wear shawls or veils as they did in Canaan some three thousand five hundred years ago. However, their very revealing, suggestive clothing now points even more plainly to the profession they practice. Among men, those who favor revolt or radical political action have also worn distinctive styles, and so do some homosexuals. Do we want to be linked up with any of these? And if we dress like them and have problems as a result—as when trying to get employment or to qualify for certain privileges in a Christian congregation—should we be surprised?

WHAT SHOULD DETERMINE HAIRSTYLES

[12] There are many styles in which you can arrange your hair. Down through the centuries, hairstyles have varied from country to country and from one period to another. Does it make any difference which hairstyle you choose? Yes, it does. Human pride has sometimes produced very extreme hairstyles. For this reason the apostles Paul and Peter found it necessary to counsel Christian women not to be extravagant or to put too much importance on hairstyles. Peter wrote: "Do not let your adornment be that of the external braiding of the hair and of the putting on of gold ornaments."—1 Peter 3:3.

[13] In recent years, however, the hairstyles of young men—especially very long hair and long sideburns—have drawn particular attention. Yet, didn't men in Bible times generally wear their hair longer than is customary in most lands today? Undoubtedly they did. But something else is equally certain. What? That men's hair was still consistently shorter than that of women. That is why the apostle Paul could write to the congregation at Corinth, Greece, and say: "Does not nature itself teach you that if a man has long hair, it is a dishonor to him; but if a woman has long hair, it is a glory to her?" (1 Corinthians 11:14, 15) How does "nature" teach us this?

[14] For one thing, among wavy-haired peoples, such as the Semites and Europeans to whom Paul was writing, there is usually a significant difference in the length that men's and women's hair

12-15. (a) What kind of hairstyles do you feel attract a lot of attention nowadays? Why do they? (b) What was the point of the counsel given at 1 Peter 3:3? (c) What does 1 Corinthians 11:14, 15 mean? How would you apply it to current trends? (d) If men imitate women in the way they wear their hair, what might this suggest to others?

will naturally grow. In most cases, the length is naturally shorter for men. At the same time, people have generally recognized that it is the "natural" thing—the proper and fitting thing— for men to cut their hair to a moderate length, shorter than that of women. For a man or a boy to wear his hair so that he looks like a girl is not natural. Rather, it is typical of an age (and lands) where homosexuality is on the increase. And the Bible shows that homosexuality is "contrary to nature," both unfitting and detestable in God's sight.—Romans 1:26, 27.

[15] Does this severely limit us? No, for just as with clothes, so with hairstyles there is a wide variety of ways of arranging one's hair that are pleasing and attractive without being immodest or unnatural. There can still be refreshing variety without going beyond the bounds of what is right in God's eyes.

WHAT ABOUT COSMETICS?

[16] The Bible shows that people have used cosmetics from ancient times. We know that people wear clothes, not merely to cover the body, but also to produce an attractive appearance. To make their bodily presence even more pleasant, the ancient Hebrews often used perfume. There is evidence, too, that they used certain cosmetics, particularly ointments, to combat dryness of skin and to improve their appearance.

[17] What, then, should be the guide for young women today who want to do what brings God's approval? They need to follow the good advice to do all things "with modesty and soundness

---

16-19. (a) How do you feel about the use of cosmetics? (b) What bad effects do they sometimes have? (c) How do Bible principles provide a balanced guide on this matter?

[or, healthfulness] of mind," letting the main adornment be "the secret person of the heart in the incorruptible apparel of the quiet and mild spirit, which is of great value in the eyes of God."—1 Timothy 2:9, 10; 1 Peter 3:3, 4.

[18] Of course, it is good for young girls to realize that cosmetics can often do more harm than good. They can ruin a good complexion or make a poor one worse. Besides this, cosmetics frequently mask the freshness of youth that is really of far greater beauty than the artificial effect cosmetics create.

[19] Overuse of cosmetics by girls often does no more than draw attention to weak points. Worse, it may prevent any beauty of personality (which is actually more attractive than good looks and far longer lasting) from showing through or being noticed. Overuse of cosmetics can pervert your personality in the eyes of others and, in time, can even tend to mold your personality into the cheapened image you thereby present.

FOLLOWING RIGHT GUIDELINES

[20] In God's Word there are no specific rules on these things, but, instead, fine guidelines are provided. Young people should seek to get a balanced outlook, and the Bible will help them to do that.

[21] Your parents have the natural right to set down supplementary guidelines. If the house you live in were painted with a wild or weird combination of colors, people would wonder if the head of the house, or his wife, had any sense. Or, if the house were neglected and became run down

20-22. (a) Instead of rules on dress and grooming, what do we find in the Bible? So, what is required of us in order to apply these? (Proverbs 2:10, 11) (b) Why do parents have the right to set out supplementary guidelines for their children?

in appearance, they would have little respect for the house owner. You represent your parents even more than the house does. You bear their name and, just as what you do and say reflects on the training they give you and the kind of people they are, so does the way you look. More importantly, if you claim to be one of God's servants you also represent Him. Does your appearance fit your claim?

²² Think of Jesus' words: "If you know these things, happy you are *if you do them*." (John 13:17) Are you able to discern for yourself the sense of what the Bible counsels? You can show that you have real insight and strength of personality by putting the Bible's counsel to work in your life. Then you will have the happiness of knowing that you are pleasing in the sight of God, his Son, and all who love and serve him.

CHAPTER 8

What Kind of Friends Do You Want?

HAVING a true friend adds a lot to the joy of living. People who are "loners" and avoid others are rarely, if ever, really happy. What is there about friendship that adds so much to your happiness?

2 Doing something with a friend seems to multiply the enjoyment of that particular experience. Jesus once told of a shepherd who found his lost sheep and of a woman who found her lost coin. Each one called in friends, saying, "Rejoice with me." (Luke 15:6, 9) Yes, you normally want to share good things with companions, and your delight seems to double as a result. Haven't you experienced that?

3 On the other hand, when things don't go well and you feel depressed, a good friend can do a lot to relieve your sadness. Friends can be a real help when trouble threatens. They can warn you of danger and help you to escape it, and can encourage you when the going is hard. You probably can agree with what Proverbs 17:17 says: "A true companion is loving all the time, and is a brother that is born for when there is distress."

4 That scripture emphasizes a quality that strongly marks real friends: Loyalty. Being a friend means more than just acting friendly. A

1-5. (a) How can friendships add to your enjoyment of life? (b) How would you describe a real friend? (Proverbs 18:24)

genuine friend is loyal to you and to your best interests. Are your friends like that?

⁵ Today, most people seem more interested in outdoing their neighbor than in helping him. Even among so-called "friends" there is often a spirit of competition, not of loyalty. Many friendships last only as long as neither person is called on to make some change or to give up some selfish interest for the good of the other. In this competitive world a true friend is not easy to find.

⁶ A fine Bible example of one who had some really worthwhile friends is seen in David. You may have heard how David, after the defeat of Goliath, an immense enemy warrior, gained a fine friend in Jonathan, the son of King Saul. Jonathan, if he had been jealous, could have hated David as a possible rival for the throne of Israel. Instead, Jonathan recognized that God's favor was on David, and "Jonathan's very soul became bound up with the soul of David, and Jonathan began to love him as his own soul." (1 Samuel 18:1) Jonathan loved him for his courage and faith in Jehovah God. Jonathan himself also must have had a similar devotion to God. There couldn't be a better foundation for a mutual friendship.

⁷ You can further read about a later friend of David named Hushai, who was one of David's close associates during his kingship. The way Hushai risked his life to thwart the traitorous conspiracy of Absalom, one of David's sons, is a thrilling account to read.—See 2 Samuel 15: 10-37; 16:16–17:16.

⁸ Perhaps you have friends like these. If not,

6-8. In what ways did Jonathan and Hushai prove that they were friends of David?

how can you gain them? It will take real effort, but it is certainly worth it.

SEEKING WORTHWHILE FRIENDS

[9] There is a lot of truth in the saying that 'the only way to have a friend is to be one.' Sometimes persons feel it keenly when they are 'left out' of things by other young persons whom they may admire. Or they may have had friends only to lose them. They feel very hurt about this. Possibly they do not realize that friendship is a two-way street.

> **To have friends, you need to be a friend.**

[10] So we do well to ask ourselves: What am I doing to be friendly to others? How much sincere and unselfish interest do I take in others, and what do I do to contribute to their happiness and their good? What qualities am I cultivating that would make others feel that they would really like to have me as a friend?

[11] The kind of friends you get depends largely on the way you go about trying to find them. Some seek to win friends by spending money on them, or by inviting them to share in the enjoyment of material possessions, such as a stereo set and records or sports equipment. True, this may draw some to you. The Proverbs say, "Many are the friends of the rich person," and that

---

9-13. (a) How can a person gain worthwhile friends? Why is it unwise to try to get friends by giving or sharing material possessions? (b) As shown at Psalm 101:5-7, what kind of persons is it best to avoid as close companions?

"everybody is a companion to the man making gifts." Yes, many people act friendly when a person spends his money freely. But when the money runs out so do the "friends."—Proverbs 14:20; 19:6.

[12] Worthwhile friends cannot be "bought," either by the use of material possessions, or by flattery or by always giving in to what the other wants. Any friend that can be bought is never worth the price, however much it might be. True friends are attracted by what you are, by your qualities, not by what they can get out of you.

[13] So, while it is good to have a friendly disposition toward people, if you want genuine friends you need to be selective about those you choose as close and confidential companions. David was. He says: "Anyone of haughty eyes and of arrogant heart, him I cannot endure. My eyes are upon the faithful ones of the earth, that they may dwell with me. . . . There will dwell inside my house no worker of trickiness." (Psalm 101:5-7) Why is it so important for young people today to be selective as to close companions?

WHY A GOOD CHOICE IS VITAL

[14] It is a basic principle of social relations that you tend to become like those around you if you associate with them long enough. Your choice of friends tells a lot about what kind of person you are or are likely to become. Your close friends are bound to have a "molding" effect on you.

[15] Do you choose friends who are honest and decent, who are considerate, who have respect

---

14-16. (a) What effect do a person's friends have on him? Illustrate. (b) How will a friendship be affected if you tell the other person that you disagree with him?

for God and his Word and who have the courage to do what is right? Or are you attracted by persons who pride themselves on being able to "outsmart" others, and who, in place of genuine courage, take blind risks just to show off? Are they ready to risk sharing in immorality, or to steal or take drugs and then brag that they are 'getting away with it'? If they try to "hook" you into going along with them in something that can harm you, can they rightly be called "friends"?

[16] Remember, if you are a close companion of such persons, you will either have to go along with them or have to disagree with them. To disagree with them will probably end the "friendship." Why? Because they will look on disagreement as criticism or reproof. Usually such persons like to ridicule others, but they can't take reproof themselves. Proverbs 9:8 talks about that kind of person and then, in contrast, adds: "Give a reproof to a wise person and he will love you." Real friends can talk frankly to each other and help each other to improve or to correct themselves where needed. When you have a really good companion who thinks straight and talks straight, you have a treasure beyond price. True friends are like diamonds—precious but rare. In sad contrast, false friends are like common stones—found everywhere.

True friends are like diamonds

¹⁷ Many young people today, because of having no faith in a personal Creator or in his Word, take the attitude of "let us eat and drink, for tomorrow we are to die." That was the way men of ancient times felt who were sentenced to fight wild beasts in the arena. They had no faith in Jehovah God and his power to give life again to those faithful to him. As a young person, you are really just getting started in life. So, do you want to adopt the attitude those condemned prisoners had toward life? After describing that viewpoint of just 'living for today,' the apostle Paul went on to say: "Do not be misled. Bad associations spoil useful habits." (1 Corinthians 15:32, 33) Think about the truthfulness of that. If you seek close companionship with persons who think only of the present, you can be sure they will ruin your hopes and efforts toward gaining a lasting happy future.

¹⁸ Sometimes a young person may say that he or she associates with another of questionable ways and reputation so as to help that one. To want to help others is a fine thing. But if you go along with them in their selfish pleasures, how much help are you giving them? For example, if you saw a child in a mud puddle, would you take some soap out into the puddle and try to clean the child with it? You would only get yourself dirty as a result. You would first have to try to encourage the child to come out of the mud puddle before you could hope to do anything about cleaning him up at close range.

¹⁹ Actually, to accept a person with bad habits

17-19. (a) If you were to be a close companion of someone who did not really believe in God or the Bible, how would you be affected? (Proverbs 11:9; Genesis 34:1, 2) (b) If you really want to help such a person, what is the best way to do it?

as a close associate will often have a bad effect on that person (as well as on yourself). Why? Because it may encourage him to keep on in the same way, feeling that he can always rely on your backing him up. Wouldn't it be of far greater help to limit your association to times when you can really aid the person by pointing out good counsel and by inviting him to accompany you to places where that counsel is explained?

THE MOST IMPORTANT FRIENDS

[20] Above all, you should think seriously as to how association with persons of questionable habits may affect your relationship with God and his Son. At James 4:4 this truth is stated: 'Whoever wants to be a friend of the world is constituting himself an enemy of God.' That principle can apply to our relationship with any one person in the world just the same as to our relationship with the world as a whole. If we approve improper ways in someone or prefer that one's companionship to that of young persons who really want to please God, then do we not show ourselves to be 'friends of the world'?

[21] If you really want happiness now and in the future, by all means learn to prize the friendship of God and his Son. For thousands of years now God has been demonstrating his friendship toward those who love righteousness, developing his grand purposes to bring them everlasting life in really happy conditions. When he was on earth, God's Son proved his loyal love for right-hearted per-

---

20. How, by our choice of friends, might we actually make ourselves enemies of God?
21-23. (a) What benefits come to a person who really has God and Christ as his friends? (Romans 8:35, 38, 39) (b) How can we show that we really want them as our friends?

sons. He told his disciples: "No one has love greater than this, that someone should surrender his soul in behalf of his friends. You are my friends if you do what I am commanding you." —John 15:13, 14.

²² Unlike many who may pretend to be your friends, Jehovah God and his Son will not give up on you or abandon you because you run into difficulties. If you put your trust in them you will find that during times of trouble their help and support will really be with you.

²³ Do you really appreciate and desire these great Friends? Then show it by seeking loyal companions who accept and will live up to the obligation the apostle John wrote about when he said: "This is what the love of God means, that we observe his commandments; and yet his commandments are not burdensome." (1 John 5:3) Through thick and thin, such companions will prove to be the kind of friends worth having.

CHAPTER 9

Are You Bored at Home?

WHILE no two homes are exactly alike, the problem of boredom is common to many young people today. In the past, it doesn't seem to have been that way so much. Years ago, families did more things together and so were more close-knit. But for many young people today "home" is just a house, a place to eat and sleep.

² Is boredom ever a problem for you? If so, then it can greatly reduce your enjoyment of your home. Perhaps sometimes you feel like striking out on your own and finding an interesting life in your own way.

³ In a sense this is a natural development in youth. As you grow and develop, you naturally expand your outlook. Your curiosity grows. You are interested in trying new things, in experimenting. The question is, How are you going to express that expanded outlook? Does it have to make you bored with home or make you tired of having parental direction and control? What's the real cause of most boredom, and what's the solution for it?

ATTITUDE CAN MAKE THE DIFFERENCE

⁴ True, some homes have real problems that make peace and contentment hard to come by.

1-3. (a) What do you think contributes to the boredom in many homes today? (b) Is it necessarily wrong to develop interests outside your home?
4-6. (a) How does a person's own attitude determine to a large extent whether he is bored or not? (b) What could you personally do to improve the spirit in your home? (Philippians 2:3, 4)

But more often than not it's your own attitude that determines whether you find your homelife enjoyable or boring. Why is that? Because right within the same set of circumstances, there are some young people who manage to enjoy life, while others in the same situation are bored. The difference is that some have a better attitude about their homelife. So coping with boredom, and with many other problems, too, is largely a matter of your own attitude toward these things.

⁵ Why not look at it this way: Every family has a personality. This isn't formed by any one person, but each one contributes something to the family's composite personality. What is your family like? Is your home a warm, cheerful place? Do you enjoy one another, have interesting con-

Trouble at sea calls for full cooperation. Do you help to steer a peaceful course when there are troubles at home?

versations at mealtimes, find pleasure in doing things together and for one another? Or do you each go your separate way, with little or no interest in one another? Which way would you prefer it to be?

6 It's easy to blame others if things aren't the way you would like them to be. But before complaining, why not first ask: "What do I myself contribute to the family personality and spirit? How much effort do I put forth to bring improvement?" If a ship is straining through stormy seas, it doesn't help much for a sailor to sit in the corner complaining. It's a case of "all hands on deck" and of everyone's lending a hand to keep the ship going through the rough seas to the desired haven.

7 Often bored young persons simply fail to see the value of the things they are given to do. Whatever assignments you have, whether at school or at home or at work, try to see how they affect your life, also the lives of others, both now and in the days to come. If you can do that, you will be able to work at those assignments with a sense of purpose. This can make the difference between enjoying life and being bored.

8 Really, the very jobs you find boring could build in you the very qualities and habits that will play the largest part in your future success in life. To illustrate: If you're a young man, have you ever built a model airplane? First, you had to put the many pieces of the frame together and then cover that frame. The frame might not even show in the final product. But without the

---

7-9. What can help us to overcome boredom in any task that we may have to do?

strength and design it gave, the airplane would be useless. Or, if you're a young woman, have you ever made a dress? The seams you sewed may not have showed when the dress was done. But without those hidden stitches, there would have been no dress.

[9] Likewise with so much that you learn at school or learn by what you do at home. It's part of an overall pattern that can help to lay the foundation for future success. By doing simple and often unexciting jobs or chores, even repeatedly, you can learn endurance and determination, and gain inner strength.

INITIATIVE AND A WIDER INTEREST

[10] Often the complaint is heard during periods of free time, "There's nothing to do." More often than not, the problem is not a lack of interesting and worthwhile things to do, but a lack of initiative, imagination and thought. Or the complaint may show we have a very narrow field of things that interest us.

[11] The present system doesn't do much to encourage initiative, especially at home. Even young people today are accustomed to be spectators rather than active participants. Is that how you spend most of the time at home, looking at movies, television programs, listening to recorded music or watching others play in some sports contest?

[12] This is a lot easier than doing things yourself, or learning how to do things. But in the long run it also contributes to boredom. It makes you very dependent on others for entertainment;

10-12. (a) When a person says, "There's nothing to do," what is usually lacking on the part of that individual? (b) What kind of recreation contributes to that lack?

it leaves you unable to do things yourself to make life interesting. This is all right for babies—but not for maturing young men and women.

[13] How broad is your field of interest? The list of worthwhile activities and fields of knowledge to be explored is almost limitless. Reading takes more effort than watching television. But it pays far higher dividends. There is no field of activity, no skill or trade, no place or people or animal that is not covered in books. And the more you read the greater your enjoyment of reading becomes, the greater your ability to absorb knowledge. But reading just to 'kill time' is not enough. You need to decide what is going to be of value. Then you can read with a goal in mind, one that can enrich your life right now as well as in the future by equipping you to *do* things.

[14] Of course, not everyone enjoys doing the things that others enjoy. Some enjoy learning to work with wood or metal, while others prefer photography or gardening. Some girls may like cooking or baking, while others prefer sewing or hairdressing. But learning to do new things, at home or elsewhere, and developing the ability to do *quality* work will bring satisfaction and keep life interesting.

[15] When you find it hard to get enthusiastic about doing something in your own interest, why not do something for someone else, starting at home? A task that might not appeal if you did

---

13, 14. What are some activities that you enjoy and that require initiative or participation on your part?

15-18. (a) How is a person's own life affected when he makes it a practice to do things for other people? (Acts 20:35) (b) What is one of the most worthwhile things that a Christian youth can do for other people? (Matthew 24:14; 1 Timothy 4:16) (c) In any worthwhile endeavor, why is perseverance important?

it for yourself can take on real interest when you do it for another—a family member, a friend, particularly someone in need. This is deeply satisfying, and there is no end of opportunities. Don't wait to be asked to do something. When what you do is unexpected by the other person, the added element of surprise will greatly add to your enjoyment. Try it out.

[16] Here's another way you can benefit by doing things for others. Young people who are genuinely thrilled at God's promise of a new order find that sharing this good news with others gives added meaning to their lives. To find persons who are hungry for truth and to be able to help them is richly rewarding. Though these are outnumbered by those who reject the truth, this does not dull the stimulating effect of this activity. Instead it makes it more challenging. It calls for endurance and faith. These are big factors in conquering boredom.

[17] The apostle Paul says of our service to God and to those who serve him: "Let us not give up in doing what is fine, for in due season we shall reap if we do not tire out." (Galatians 6:9) Similarly, when you seek to develop abilities that have some real purpose and value, you should persevere until you begin to harvest some of the fruits of your labors.

[18] Then, as time goes on, you can broaden your exploration of still other abilities to develop, and you will become a better, more interesting and worthwhile person as a result. Your parents and others at home will be glad to have you around, and you will be free from being bored at home.

CHAPTER 10

How Do You View Your Parents?

WHEN others tell you how they feel about their parents, they are also telling you something about themselves. Yes, what you say and do toward your parents reveals what is in your own mind and heart. It tells a lot about the kind of person you are right now. It also gives a clear indication of the kind of person you are likely to become in the future. This is because behavior patterns that you develop at home gradually become a part of you.

[2] Some young people develop a negative attitude toward their parents in nearly everything. Many feel that their parents never understand them or even try to, that they are hopelessly old-fashioned and cannot offer any useful guidance in this fast-moving world. This feeling soon grows into a general attitude of rebellion. If not curbed, it easily becomes a habit. It will show itself in dealings with people outside the family circle. And before you know where you are, it can also lead you into serious trouble because of an unwillingness to obey laws designed for the benefit and protection of human society.

[3] Yet there are others who do not feel and act that way. They grow up to view their parents

---

1-3. (a) What does a person's attitude toward his parents tell about him? (b) What attitude do the young folks you know have toward their parents? Do you agree with them? (c) What kind of training can help a young person to respect his parents, and why?

with respect. These young persons know why the world is in so much trouble and what the future holds for them. So they are not pressured into conforming to the negative attitude that others have. They appreciate that their parents have instilled in them respect for the highest principles of human behavior—those found in the inspired written Word of God. As the Bible counsels: "And you, fathers, do not be irritating your children, but go on bringing them up in the discipline and mental-regulating of Jehovah." These youths have responded to that training, and willingly play their part. As a result, they appreciate their place in the family arrangement. A good relationship exists in the home.—Ephesians 6:4.

OBEDIENCE DUE PARENTS

⁴ But what about those whose parents do not attempt to teach them Bible principles? Does this mean they do not have to give their parents respect and obedience? While it is true that parental guidance is bound to suffer as it gets away from God's standards, this doesn't lessen the need for these youths to develop a good attitude toward their parents. Why not? There are several reasons.

⁵ Having never been on your own, you may not fully appreciate all that your parents have done for you. But stop and think: Since your birth, your father and mother have cared for you daily. They have provided food and clothing, and a home to live in, and have seen to your education.

⁶ If you had to hire someone to do what your parents have done for you since your birth, it

---

4-6. (a) What have your parents done for you thus far in life? (b) How can you show that you appreciate it? (Ephesians 6:1, 2)

would cost you a small fortune. Your parents deserve respect for all of that. Later, if you marry and become a parent, you will more fully appreciate how much your parents did for you. But why not show appreciation now? If you pay back some of the love you owe your parents by giving them respect and obedience, then you show that you are developing into a mature person, one who has good sense, one who values those who do him good.

⁷ This is not to say that your parents are perfect. Of course they make mistakes. But so do you. Likely you make many more, since you don't have their experience in life. Do you criticize your parents for their mistakes, yet expect them not to say anything about yours? To be consistent, you should learn to overlook mistakes they make, just as they have to overlook many that you make. And since they have the far heavier responsibility, it is understandable that they may fall short sometimes. The Bible principle holds good: "The one that does not practice mercy will have his judgment without mercy. Mercy exults triumphantly over judgment."—James 2:13.

⁸ However, what you consider to be a parental mistake in some cases may simply be a viewpoint that differs from yours. When this is so, and your parents have taken a definite stand on the matter at issue, what should you do?

⁹ You need to keep in mind that the position of your parents is not the same as yours. A parent

7-12. (a) How should a young person view mistakes made by his parents? (Matthew 6:14, 15) (b) As shown in the Bible, what position has God given to parents? (Proverbs 6:20) Why is this a necessary arrangement? (c) How serious a matter is it to disobey one's parents?

Do you give your parents the respect they deserve?

represents someone higher in God's arrangement of things. God has given your parents authority and responsibility that you do not have as yet. Hence, final decisions in matters affecting you belong to your parents. That is why God's Word counsels: "You children, be obedient to your parents in everything, for this is well-pleasing in the Lord." Of course, this means obedience to everything your parents require that does not violate God's laws.—Colossians 3:20.

¹⁰ You see, there has to be order in human society. Without order, there would be confusion, even anarchy. For example, a sailor doesn't dic-

tate to the captain how to run the ship, nor does a ball player tell the manager how to handle the ball club. It is true that a good captain and a good manager welcome and, in fact, encourage suggestions from those under their direction. However, if they allowed others to order them around and dictate what should be done, their authority would soon be undermined, and confusion and disorder would result. Don't you agree?

[11] So, too, there has to be order in the family circle. And there God has assigned the father as the head, with the mother cooperating closely. Both parents have been appointed as supervisors of their children. So when your parents place certain requirements on you, such as the time you must be indoors at night, with whom you can associate, the way you groom yourself, and so forth, and you obey them, then you are respecting God's arrangement. When you disobey your parents, you are disrespecting the arrangement of God. That means clashing with God, the Creator of both you and your parents! And you know who will be the loser there. So, how you respond to the direction of your parents reflects how you feel about the One who is higher than they are and to whom they are under obligation to submit, Jehovah God.

[12] That is why God's Word says: "The eye that holds a father in derision and that despises obedience to a mother—the ravens of the torrent valley will pick it out and the sons of the eagle will eat it up." Yes, a wrong attitude toward parents may cost youths their lives.—Proverbs 30:17.

LESSONS LEARNED FROM SUBORDINATION

[13] Someday, when you are of legal age and perhaps have a family of your own, wouldn't you want your children to give you respect and obedience? But if you haven't learned how to do that with your own parents, is it likely that you will train your children very successfully in their giving such respect? You reap what you sow, says the Bible. (Galatians 6:7) Learn how to cope with the subordinate position you are in now, and that will help you to cope with the greater responsibility of adulthood, and perhaps parenthood, later on.

[14] Also, if you develop a negative attitude toward your parents, it can show up in other things you do later. For instance, if you work for an employer, will you always resent his authority over you? When he gives you something to do, will you find it difficult to comply? Will you constantly complain about your work? And what about your attitude toward those with whom you work? You may find yourself always complaining about them, never thanking them for the good things they may do for you. Or if you go to school to learn a trade, or are being trained on the job, after a few weeks you may begin to feel that you know more than your instructor. All these attitudes may easily cause you much grief and trouble. They can be the fruitage of having developed the wrong attitude toward your parents in the first place.

[15] Hence, accept the reality of family life and

13-17. (a) How can your learning to respect and obey your parents help you when you become a parent? (b) How can it help you at school and when you work for an employer? (c) More importantly, how will it affect your standing with God?

your position in it. Appreciate that it is God's way, and that his way is the very best.

[16] But if you refuse to accept your proper place in the family during your teen-age years, then you are asking for trouble. Not only will it affect your relationship with your parents and others, as well as your later life; far more importantly, it will impair your standing with God. And he is the one who determines whether you will live forever in his new order, or will pass out of existence when this wicked system of things is soon destroyed. Respond to the appeal: "My son, my law do not forget, and my commandments may your heart observe, because length of days and years of life and peace will be added to you." —Proverbs 3:1, 2.

[17] Just think of the reward that persons will receive who observe the commandments of our heavenly Father and who don't forget His law. The reward is *"length of days and years of life and peace."* Is that what you want? Do you desire to live a long time, and really enjoy a peaceful, happy life? Then prove that you do by listening to God's encouragement to be obedient to your parents.

CHAPTER 11

Why Study in School?

WHY do you go to school? Perhaps where you live you have to go to school up to a certain age; there is no choice. Or perhaps you are still a minor and so you have to do what your parents direct.

2 However, do you personally see any other reasons for being in school? Are there any benefits that come from applying yourself while at school or from doing homework? You likely know many young people who study just enough to get by, even if that—right? Yet, by not taking advantage of the opportunity to learn, they usually handicap themselves for the rest of their lives. Why?

3 Because what a person does during his youth has a great bearing on what he can do as an adult. Even regarding school the Bible principle applies: "Whatever a man is sowing, this he will also reap." (Galatians 6:7) But, you might ask, what are some of the benefits from 'sowing' time and effort in school study now?

PRACTICAL TRAINING

4 You have to face the fact that before many more years, you may have to support yourself. You may eventually take on the obligations of a

1-3. (a) How do you feel about school? (b) In what way does the Bible principle at Galatians 6:7 apply to schooling?
4-6. (a) Why is a person better off if he makes good use of opportunities to learn while in school? (Proverbs 21:5) (b) What courses that are offered at school do you think would be most helpful to you later in life?

80

husband and father, or a wife and mother. Would you like to make those responsibilities easier, more enjoyable? You can if you take advantage of your school years, learning things that will be useful in your adult life.

⁵ In many schools there are courses that teach you the fundamentals of different skills. For young men, there may be classes in carpentry, installing electrical equipment, welding, accounting and others. Young women can take courses in secretarial work, homemaking arts, such as cooking and sewing, and other valuable subjects.

⁶ Much of this training may not be easily available after you leave school. If you get it later, you might even find it costly. Or you might have to learn it by working with others who perhaps

Practical instruction can prepare you for later life

have little interest in teaching you. So, while still at school, why not take the opportunity to learn some of these things? And when it comes time for school courses to be selected, by all means talk the matter over with your parents. In this way you'll be able to benefit from their experience in life.

LEARN TO READ WELL

[7] While there are many things of practical value that you can learn in school, there is one that can bring you much joy. And it will have a tremendous influence on the rest of your school life and your entire adult life as well. It is the ability to read—and to read WELL. It is the key to unlocking many kinds of knowledge, skills and enjoyment.

[8] In your waking hours you daily face things to read: signs, labels, books, magazines, newspapers, forms, also letters. All of this can be an unpleasant chore for those who read poorly. However, if you learn to read well, you will find your life greatly enriched in a pleasurable way.

[9] Especially if you are a Christian will you want to learn to read well, so you can learn what is in God's Word, the Bible. You will also find skillful reading to be of great value when talking to others about God's purposes. Yes, good reading and good talking are closely linked.

[10] Don't be discouraged if, like many, you find you have a problem in reading. It is mainly a matter of practice, and being alert to note the way words are spelled. Read aloud at times. This will help you to get the correct meaning and to

7-11. (a) Why is the ability to read well especially valuable? (1 Timothy 4:13; Joshua 1:8) (b) What could help you to improve your reading ability?

express the proper feeling when you read. And, if possible, ask someone who reads well to listen to you. That will help you to correct any mistakes or any bad habits you are developing.

[11] True, the ability to read with ease and fluency doesn't come without real effort. But for the effort you put forth now you will be repaid many times. It will aid you to get the best out of life.

OTHER BENEFITS FROM STUDYING

[12] Some school subjects may not seem to be of much practical value, but they help to broaden your outlook and can be useful in other ways. Studying history, geography and languages enables you to learn about other peoples and places. Mathematics, which is considered a difficult subject by many, is very useful in many trades and occupations. It is even valuable to a homemaker who needs to figure out recipes and to keep budgets.

[13] There is another benefit to studying in school, even those subjects you don't like. Study exercises your mind and improves your ability to use it. It is something like a muscle in your body—the more you exercise it the better it will serve you. You will find that mental effort gradually becomes easier and more productive. But, as with a muscle, the mind will get "flabby" if you don't bother to use it much. Who would want his mind to be like that?

[14] Is there anything else of particular value that comes from applying yourself to your studies in school? Yes, you can learn self-discipline. This may not appeal to you now. But, as you know,

---

12-14. (a) Of what practical value are the courses that you are taking in school right now? (b) How will disciplining yourself to study prove of value to you later in life?

you can't always do just the things you prefer to do in life. That will be even more true when the time comes for you to take on greater responsibilities in making your own living, or in caring for your own family. If, like a skilled athlete, you get used to disciplining yourself now, it will help you to acquire the discipline needed to face adult obligations. It will also help you to develop the ability to *concentrate*. That is something so many people wish they had learned to develop when they were young.

A PROTECTION

15 As regards applying yourself diligently to your studies, there is yet another benefit that deserves special mention. Diligence in study can serve as a protection to you. In what way?

16 More than likely you've seen evidences of moral problems among your schoolmates. There is much sexual immorality and taking of drugs, with very sad results. Also, a spirit of rebellion prevails among many youths.

17 It may bother you a lot to be in company with people who have no respect for the fine standards of conduct taught in God's Word. Although you can't avoid contacting such persons, you can avoid associating with them beyond what is necessary for your schoolwork. And if you pay good attention to your studies, that will fill a sizable portion of your free time after school, automatically limiting your association with unprincipled persons. Seeing your desire to get on

---

15-18. (a) In what way can diligence in study be a protection to you? (Proverbs 13:20) (b) Why should a young person who is a Christian especially want to set a fine example in school? (Titus 2:6, 7, 10) (c) What life prospect that Christians have should be a strong incentive to you to study and to acquire practical skills in school? (1 John 2:15-17; 2 Peter 3:13)

with your education, persons of that type, in time, will likely leave you alone. This will be a protection to you.

[18] Then, too, if you are known as a true Christian, by applying yourself in your schoolwork you will set a fine example. That will be a credit to you, to your parents and to the God you worship. As a young Christian, you will find great encouragement and incentive in this fact: Many of the abilities and skills you develop now will be useful beyond the duration of this present system of things. Why? Because the Bible proves that this entire wicked system is nearing its end. Soon now it will be replaced by God's righteous new order where honest-hearted persons will be able to enjoy everlasting life. In that new order God's promise will prove true: "The work of their own hands my chosen ones will use to the full." (Isaiah 65:22) So the good study and work habits you learn now as a youth can prove to be a source of satisfaction and enjoyment forever.

CHAPTER 12

Do You Finish
What You Start?

MUCH of human happiness comes through accomplishment. For instance, if you decide to learn to play a guitar and you keep at it until you can, then you get enjoyment from it. But if you quit soon after starting, you never get that pleasure and satisfaction. The same is true of any undertaking that requires practice and training, covering a period of time.

² However, in this matter of sticking with a project until it is finished, there are certain tendencies we all have to outgrow or overcome.

PROBLEMS INVOLVED

³ As you know, little children have a very short attention span. Even in play it isn't long before they are easily distracted or lose interest. But as a person grows, powers of concentration develop. You may have noted that in yourself. To a large degree you have to cultivate this quality, but it's surely worth it because it helps you to get so much more out of life.

⁴ To concentrate means that you have to overcome another common trait. That is *impatience.*

1, 2. In order to have the satisfaction that comes with accomplishment, what is required of you?
3-8. (a) What can help a person to overcome impatience? (b) Before you ever start on a project, what is it wise to do? Whose counsel could benefit you in deciding? (c) Under what circumstances might it be better not to finish what you have started?

Think back to when you were a small child. As you remember, little children always want things NOW! Often when they try to do something and do not succeed after a few attempts, they are ready to quit. Well, you probably know many teenagers who are still like that. But if you appreciate that some of the most worthwhile things in life take time and effort, it will help you not to give up easily.

⁵ An impatient person usually undertakes things hastily, on impulse. A wise proverb tells us: "The plans of the diligent one surely make for advantage, but everyone that is hasty surely heads for want." (Proverbs 21:5) So, before you embark on some project or accept some assignment or job, first of all make sure it is something genuinely worth while.

⁶ In some cases the wise thing to do is *not* to finish what you start. How so? Because perhaps it was a bad idea from the beginning. The goal may be a wrong one, one that is out of harmony with right principles. Or, it may not be a good one for *you*. Is it worth the time and effort that it will take to reach it? Do you have good reason to believe you *can* reach it?

⁷ Jesus told of the man who sets out to build a tower without first figuring out the cost and whether he can meet it or not. As Jesus said, the man may lay the foundation and then find that he can go no farther, causing observers to laugh and say: "This man started to build but was not able to finish." (Luke 14:28-30) So, if you want to finish what you start, *count the cost beforehand.*

[8] Weigh advantages against disadvantages. Ask others their opinion, especially your parents. Benefit from their experience; they have made mistakes and can steer you away from these. The Bible is an outstanding source of wise and practical counsel. It is from God and it sets forth lessons learned by people over a span of thousands of years. For example, King Solomon did about all a man can do in the way of seeking pleasure in purely material things. He tells us the result: It was just a "striving after wind." So why take up a similar worthless pursuit?—Ecclesiastes 2:3-11.

AVOID BECOMING A QUITTER

[9] Once you are convinced that your goal is really worth while, planning *how* to reach it is also vital. Many young persons fail to finish what they start because they become discouraged. Some unforeseen problems or obstacles may spring up. Or they find that what they undertook to do is harder than what they thought it would be. What now?

[10] Such a situation reveals what you are really made of. If you let hardships fill you with negative and pessimistic thoughts, this will rob you of the strength to go on. It is just as the Bible proverb says: "Have you shown yourself discouraged in the day of distress? Your power will be scanty." (Proverbs 24:10) So, instead, look on the situation as a *challenge*. Rise to meet it with extra effort —extra thought, energy and time. Challenges can

---

9-12. (a) Once you have selected a goal, why is it good to plan how you are going to reach it? (b) When you encounter problems, how should these be viewed? (c) Why is it important not to get in the habit of being a quitter? (Luke 9:62)

make life interesting if you do not run away from them. By overcoming, you grow in confidence and resourcefulness. You can then undertake future tasks with greater assurance and enjoyment.

[11] So avoid developing the habit of quitting just because the going gets hard. Otherwise, the next time things get difficult, the tendency will be to do the same, to "throw in the towel," to quit. By not letting this habit get a start, you can keep your life from becoming just a series of failures and unfinished projects.

[12] If you prove that you are not one who gives up easily, not a quitter or a dropout, you will earn the confidence and respect of others. While yet a young man, the early Christian Timothy was "well reported on by the brothers" in two different towns. (Acts 16:2) That is why the apostle Paul selected him as a traveling companion. Timothy had unique privileges, going with the apostle throughout many parts of the Roman Empire. After about a dozen years of faithful service, sometimes in dangerous situations, he was entrusted with weighty responsibility, which he carried out despite not having the best of health. Yes, Timothy could be relied on to stay with his assignment and do thorough work. He was a man to be trusted. But it took time and perseverance to merit that trust.

BASIS FOR PERSEVERANCE

[13] If you are seeking to do something because it is right or out of a desire to please God, then he will help you to see it through. Consider Noah,

---

13, 14. (a) How have we benefited from Noah's perseverance in building the ark? (b) What can we learn from the apostle Paul's example of perseverance? (2 Timothy 4:16, 17)

for example. The ark that he and his sons built was a three-story chestlike structure over four hundred feet (122 meters) long. It was no "weekend project." But because he saw the job through to its finish, Noah and his family survived the deluge and we, his descendants, are alive today.

[14] Again, consider the apostle Paul. He was a real example of one who did not give up when matters got difficult. To him, his particular assignment of service was worth enduring all manner of hardship for in order to retain it to its finish. He was willing to undergo beatings, stoning, imprisonment, hard labor, sleepless nights, thirst, hunger, cold and lack of clothing, dangers from enemies of the truth and from common criminals, also from wild beasts and the forces of nature as he traveled over land and sea. Because he was not a quitter, he could truthfully say he had 'fought the fine fight, run the course to the finish, observed the faith.' On what basis? Not because of self-confidence, but as Paul himself said: "For all things I have the strength by virtue of him who imparts power to me." And as he also wrote: "We are coming off completely victorious through him that loved us." (2 Timothy 4:6-8; Philippians 4:13; Romans 8:35-39) Wouldn't you say he was a person worth imitating?

[15] To enjoy life you must also be able to get on well with others, get their cooperation and win their respect. You cannot do this if you are quick to "give up" on people, starting friendships and then dropping them at the first sign of disagree-

---

15. (a) Why do we all need to be able to get along well with other people? (b) What will help us to avoid being quick to "give up" on others when they disappoint us?

ment. Examine yourself. Do you sometimes handle your relations with others poorly, so that they may have reason to take offense? Well, does this cause you to "give up" on yourself? Then why be quick to get irritated or lose interest in others because they may sometimes disappoint you? Take the time needed to work out problems with patience. Who cannot see the wisdom of the proverb: "He that is slow to anger is abundant in discernment, but one that is impatient is exalting foolishness"?—Proverbs 14:29.

[16] The rewards of perseverance are many and well worth the effort. By proving yourself a person who sees things through to the finish, you gain many privileges and benefits. Jesus said of those following him: "He that has endured to the end is the one that will be saved." (Matthew 24:13) As Christians, we are in a race. The grand prize is everlasting life. You will gain that prize only if you develop the ability to persevere in spite of problems or hardships and see things through.

---

16. How is our developing perseverance involved in our getting the fulfillment of our Christian hope?

CHAPTER 13

How Do You View Discipline?

YOU probably know someone—maybe a fellow student or even a teacher—who never admits to making a mistake or being wrong. How do you feel about someone like that? Would your opinion of him go up or down if one day he came right out and said, "I'm sorry; I see I was wrong"?

² Really, we all make mistakes, don't we? None of us are perfect or faultless. The Bible tells us that. It shows that, due to our first parent Adam's disobedience, all men are born with an inheritance of imperfection, sin. The Bible explains that "through one man [Adam] sin entered into the world and death through sin, and thus death spread to all men because they had all sinned." —Romans 5:12.

³ Some mistakes come from just 'not knowing.' But not all do. Many mistakes are because of *not caring*. For example, a passenger in an airplane might pay no attention when the stewardess explains the use of life jackets or of the plane's oxygen supply. If, as a result, the passenger failed to make use of these provisions in an emergency and lost his life, it would not be simply because he didn't know. Rather, he didn't *care* to know.

⁴ So not all wrongs can be chalked up to simple error. Willful ignorance is often the cause. Worse, a person may do what he knows is wrong—excusing himself for one reason or another.

1-4. (a) Why are we all prone to make mistakes? (b) Besides lack of knowledge, what else gives rise to mistakes?

[5] All of this shows the need for discipline, which involves correction. We *all* need correction, whether we are young or old. In fact, if there were no discipline or correction there could be no progress in any field of human living. People would keep on making the same mistakes, believing the same wrong ideas, never advancing in knowledge or ability.

[6] But did you know that discipline means more than just correction? It can also be training that molds, strengthens, or makes better. Discipline is properly given with a view to correction and improvement for the future.

WHY HARD TO TAKE

[7] But if discipline is so beneficial, why do most persons find it so hard to take? It's really for the same reason that causes us to need discipline in the first place, namely, our imperfection. Discipline can easily make us feel embarrassed or it may hurt our pride. Note, however, the other side of the picture as explained by the apostle Paul: "True, no discipline seems for the present to be joyous, but grievous; yet afterward to those who have been trained by it it yields peaceable fruit, namely, righteousness."—Hebrews 12:11.

[8] Humility takes most of the sting out of discipline. However, many persons let pride and stubbornness cause them to resist discipline. But when the correction or reproof is well founded, the person who stubbornly rejects it simply makes himself look foolish in the eyes of others. God's

5, 6. (a) Why is correction beneficial to both young and old? (b) What is the objective of discipline? (Proverbs 1:1-4)
7-9. (a) Why is discipline often hard to take? (b) How can this be overcome?

Word says: "Wisdom and discipline are what mere fools have despised."—Proverbs 1:7.

[9] In contrast, we read: "Give a reproof to a wise person and he will love you." Why? Because he knows that through correction "he will become still wiser."—Proverbs 9:8, 9.

HOW WILL YOU REACT?

[10] The real question is: What do you want to do with your life? Do you just want to drift along? Or are you willing to work toward a worthwhile future? How do you view this matter? Do you agree with God's Word, which advises: "Listen to counsel and accept discipline, in order that you may become wise in your future"? —Proverbs 19:20.

[11] Whatever your viewpoint, sometime in life you are bound to receive discipline. And you will find it more pleasant and easy to take if you keep in mind that it is God's arrangement. He provides discipline because he loves us and wants to help us to improve. So the Bible says that anyone who hates discipline is, in effect, 'throwing God's words behind him.'—Psalm 50:17.

[12] Discipline rightly comes from an authorized source. Who do you believe is in the best position to administer discipline to younger persons? God has assigned that job to parents, for they are responsible for their children's lives. And, within the Christian congregation, God has provided spiritually "older men" who are "able both to exhort by the teaching that is healthful and to reprove those who contradict."—Titus 1:5-9.

10-12. (a) As shown at Proverbs 19:20, how can discipline affect our lives? (b) Why does God discipline us? (Hebrews 12:5, 6) (c) Who is authorized to give us discipline?

¹³ How do you react to discipline from your parents? Many youths resent it, at least for a time, even to the point of leaving home on that account. If you are upset over someone's giving you counsel or reproof, stop and ask yourself: Why did they take the time and effort to do it? In most cases, though not all, you know that giving reproof is not exactly pleasant for them. They do it because they *care* enough about you to make the effort. That alone should make you think seriously about what they say.

¹⁴ True, it takes strength to face up to our mistakes. And it takes humility to accept dis-

---

13-17. If we are inclined to resent discipline, what thoughts might we call to mind that can help us to readjust our thinking? (Proverbs 4:1. 2; 13:24; 15:32)

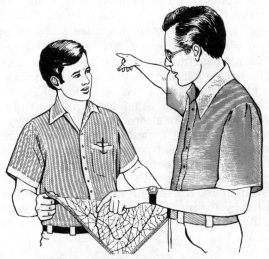

When you are given correction, how do you react?

cipline, especially if you feel that it was not called for. But if you take it quietly and do not kick against it, you will likely profit by it, and this will ease the situation.

[15] Remember, too, that those offering discipline likely are not trying to "hobble" you so that you are cramped in walking life's highway. Rather, they probably are trying to help you to make progress. Wise discipline protects against harmful accidents, keeps you free from things that will tie you up with problems, making your way difficult. If you accept correction, the Bible promises: "When you walk, your pace will not be cramped; and if you run, you will not stumble. Take hold on discipline; do not let go. Safeguard it, for it itself is your life."—Proverbs 4:10-13.

[16] Of course, you don't need to wait for others to correct you. You can practice self-discipline. By being alert, you can recognize many of your own mistakes and take steps to correct them.

[17] Many benefits come from being receptive to discipline. To admit mistakes in a straightforward way gives you a better feeling inside. It strengthens your heart and mind for what is right. It makes for good relations with others; they accept you as being honest, humble and balanced, refreshingly different from so many others today. Above all, it is essential for bringing you into a good relationship with Jehovah God and keeping you there. It also can assure you of a lasting and happy future. Yes, "the reproofs of discipline are the way of life."—Proverbs 6:23.

CHAPTER 14

Should You Drink
Alcoholic Beverages?

MORE and more, young persons are facing this question today. Why? Because the use of alcohol has been growing among teen-agers, with many turning to it in place of drugs. In view of this, let's examine some facts, and see if they can help us in looking at this matter sensibly, for our own lasting good.

[2] Alcoholic beverages—that covers a wide range. Some drinks, such as beer, have quite a low alcohol content. Others are a bit stronger, as is true of most table wines. Then there are what are called "distilled spirits," with high alcohol content. These include brandies, whiskeys, gin, vodka and others.

[3] Regional attitudes and customs are also of wide variety. In some lands—France, Italy, Spain, Greece and other countries—wine is a common beverage at the family table. This may have developed because of a problem in obtaining good water supplies or may just be due to custom. But even in these lands the attitude toward the use of alcoholic beverages will vary. Not only this, but the results from using alcoholic beverages also vary from country to country and from person to person. You need to keep this in mind

---

1-4. (a) Do any of the young folks with whom you are acquainted use alcoholic beverages? (b) How do people in our area feel about the use of alcoholic drinks? Is the use of such drinks viewed the same everywhere?

in developing a sensible viewpoint toward such beverages.

⁴ Well, then, in view of all this variety, is there any stable, consistent standard to guide you in this matter? Yes, the Bible provides this. In noting what it says, see if you don't agree that it is wise and balanced advice.

A BALANCED VIEWPOINT

⁵ The Bible shows that from ancient times wine was a common beverage with meals, being used by such persons as Abraham, Isaac and many others. Jesus provided wine for a wedding feast, and the apostle Paul counseled Timothy to "use a little wine for the sake of your stomach and your frequent cases of sickness."—1 Timothy 5:23.

⁶ Rightfully, the Bible lists wine as among God's provisions and blessings for the enjoyment of humans. A Bible psalm says: "He is making green grass sprout for the beasts, and vegetation for the service of mankind, . . . and wine that makes the heart of mortal man rejoice." (Psalm 104:14, 15) The Bible also shows that God's people sometimes used other alcoholic beverages, including beer and liquor.

⁷ Does this mean there is no need for caution on your part as to drinking alcoholic beverages? By no means. For God's Word shows the 'other side of the coin' as well. There are many things in life that are not wrong in themselves but that can bring serious consequences if misused or used too soon. God gave humans procreative

---

5-7. (a) What does the Bible say about the use of wine among God's people in times past? (b) Could you give an illustration showing how a thing that is good can cause serious problems if misused or used too soon?

powers, but these are to be used only in honorable marriage and their use can bring the heavy responsibility of caring for a family. Fire, steam, electricity and various tools can be very helpful to men and women in their work, but, used carelessly, they can also be very harmful. The drinking of alcoholic beverages, too, can have serious effects if caution is not exercised.

EFFECT OF ALCOHOL

8 Consider the effects of alcohol on the human system. Unlike other substances, it needs no digestion. It begins to be absorbed into your bloodstream as soon as it enters the stomach, though most absorption takes place in the small intestine. It is quickly carried to your brain, your liver and other parts of the body. Since alcohol contains calories, your body sets about metabolizing it, that is, transforming the alcohol into a chemical form that your body can, in effect, burn up as fuel. Most of this work is done by the liver. Your lungs and kidneys lighten some of the load as they expel some of the alcohol through the breath and urine.

9 Once in the bloodstream, what effect does alcohol have on a person? In small amounts, the effect is that of mild sedation, relaxation or tranquillity. In larger amounts it depresses the brain's 'switchboard controls.' So it may, at least in some people, cause a person to become very talkative, excessively active and even aggressive. Haven't you seen that happen to people?

10 With still greater concentrations of alcohol,

8-11. (a) When taken into the body, what effect does a small amount of alcohol have? What happens as the amounts become larger? (b) How does Proverbs 23:29-35 describe the effects of drunkenness? Have you ever seen anyone act like that?

the brain becomes severely depressed. The central nervous system is affected. And the individual begins to have difficulty in coordinating his movements. That is why he has trouble in walking, seeing and speaking clearly. He also becomes confused in his thinking. The problem is made worse by the peculiar effect alcohol has in making the person imagine that his senses are really operating better than usual. So, he is generally the last one to realize that he has taken too much. And once he reaches the point of intoxication, only time can bring any relief.

[11] Note this very accurate picture of the dangers and the discomfort that come with overindulgence in alcoholic beverages. It is found in the Bible at Proverbs 23:29-35: "Who has woe? Who has uneasiness? Who has contentions? Who has concern? Who has wounds for no reason? Who has dullness of eyes? Those staying a long time with the wine, those coming in to search out mixed wine. . . . Your own eyes will see strange things, and your own heart will speak perverse things. And you will certainly become like one lying down in the heart of the sea [experiencing confusion and helplessness like that of a drowning person], even like one lying down at the top of a mast [where the rocking back and forth of a ship is most keenly felt]. 'They have struck me, but I did not become sick; they have smitten me, but I did not know it [for a drunken person is insensible to what is going on and often is not aware of his wounds until he has become sober].'" That doesn't sound very pleasant, does it? But that is what happens when someone gets drunk.

A GROWING PROBLEM

[12] But are young people in any real danger of getting drunk or even becoming alcoholics? Yes, they are. Donald G. Phelps, director of the National Institute on Alcohol Abuse and Alcoholism in Washington, D.C., said:

> "The [ratio of] alcohol abusers among our adolescent population is about the same as among the adult population. Ten per cent of all the 13-year-old boys (interviewed in a national survey of teenagers) get drunk at least once a week. That's 52 times a year."

[13] France has for a long time faced a serious problem of alcoholism among children, some persons showing signs of cirrhosis of the liver at an early age. In Hungary (a country with one of the highest rates of suicide), medical centers in recent years have been treating thousands of children annually for intoxication.

[14] Why do young people get into this situation? In many cases there is someone in their family who is already an excessive drinker. In many other cases, it is because other young people urge them to begin drinking. Sometimes a young boy is pressured by others of his age to 'prove he is a man' by drinking a lot of some alcoholic drink, or a young girl is made to feel she is socially backward if she does not drink.

[15] But ask yourself, Does drinking an alcoholic beverage really prove anything as to the kind of person you are? Obviously not, since even animals can be induced to drink it and get drunk. Really, what do persons want who would pressure you

12-17. (a) How extensive is the problem of alcohol abuse among young folks? How do they get started? (b) If someone tries to pressure you to drink, what motive may he really have? (Habakkuk 2:15)

to drink? Are they seeking your good, something that will benefit you? Or are they just trying to put you in the same class with themselves? Might they be hoping to have the "fun" of seeing you lose control and act, not like a grown man or woman, but like a small child who cannot walk, talk or see clearly and who does and says foolish things?

[16] Note what one authority, Dr. Giorgio Lolli, said:

> "The alcoholic is retreating from the adult world into infancy, physically and psychologically. His mental perceptions and bodily sensations become indistinguishable. Like the infant, he becomes helpless and requires a baby's care."

Furthermore, persons seeking sexual immorality may also encourage a companion to drink so that his or her self-control deteriorates.

[17] Surely giving in to any of these pressures would show—not that one has strength or is grown up—but that one is weak and lacks moral courage. With good reason Proverbs 20:1 warns that wine can become "a ridiculer, intoxicating liquor is boisterous, and everyone going astray by it is not wise." You do not need to experience drunkenness to know how undesirable it is—any more than you need to break a leg to know how painful that can be.

[18] It is not merely the danger of becoming a "problem drinker" or an alcoholic that calls for caution. Just one bad experience with alcohol can bring lasting damage. It may be a serious auto accident, possibly with loss of life or limb—your own or that of some innocent person. Or it may be an act of immorality that puts a stain on your

---

18, 19. Even though a person may not be an alcoholic, what can result from just one bad experience with alcoholic drinks?

whole life and that may bring thorny complications. Or it may be some violent conduct that you will long regret. Why take an unnecessary risk?

[19] The possibility of such tragic results is clear from the fact that, of the some 50,000 persons dying each year on the highways of the United States, more than half the deaths are from accidents that have alcohol-related causes. And a New York *Times* report says that "more than 80 per cent of homicides and aggressive assaults are committed by intoxicated persons."

WEIGHING THE MATTER WITH WISDOM

[20] In weighing the matter, remember that alcoholic beverages are not one of life's essentials

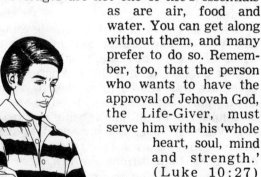

as are air, food and water. You can get along without them, and many prefer to do so. Remember, too, that the person who wants to have the approval of Jehovah God, the Life-Giver, must serve him with his 'whole heart, soul, mind and strength.' (Luke 10:27) Misuse of alcohol can, not only rob one of mental clarity and alertness and physical

20, 21. (a) Why do some persons prefer not to use any alcoholic beverages at all? (Hosea 4:11) (b) Why is it unwise to use such drinks to try to escape from problems?

strength, but also affect one's heart, leading to the development of bad motives.

²¹ True, the Bible speaks of the moderate use of such beverages as wine. But what if one looks to such alcoholic drinks as an escape from the reality of life or from boredom? Or as a personality medicine to 'brace one's nerves' in overcoming timidity or fear? He may well find that the cure is worse than the ailment. What good is money if it proves to be counterfeit? And what good is a feeling of happiness or courage if it proves to be only artificial?

²² An enlightening report by the National Institute of Mental Health* shows that dangers of the misuse of alcohol were *least likely* to appear where the following circumstances prevailed: (1) Where the individual's earliest contact with alcoholic beverages came within a strong family or religious group and where the beverages usually were of low alcohol content (such as table wines or beer) and usually taken at mealtimes as just part of the meal. (2) Where use of these beverages was viewed as neither a virtue nor a sin, drinking not being considered as any measure of adulthood or of one's being a "real man." (3) Where no one was pressured to drink and where turning down a drink was no more looked down upon than turning down a piece of bread. (4) Where drinking in excess was strongly disapproved, being considered neither "stylish" nor comical nor something to be tolerated. And, perhaps, most importantly, (5) where there was

---

* Published by the U.S. Department of Health, Education and Welfare.

22. According to one report, under what circumstances is it least likely that the use of alcoholic beverages will lead to problems?

united and consistent agreement on what is right and what is wrong as regards the use of such beverages, parents presenting a good example of moderation.

[23] Your finest and safest guide, of course, is God's Word. As we have seen, it provides examples of the proper use of alcoholic beverages and strong warnings against their misuse. It counsels young persons to respect their parents' judgment. So be wise, listen to what they say as to whether you should drink alcoholic beverages or not, or under what circumstances you may do so. You are also wise if you avoid indulging in these beverages when those partaking are all young persons, and there are no parents or relatives present to provide a guiding influence.

[24] To get the best out of your youth, and to enjoy lasting happiness, you need to look to God's Word for guidance. So, "whether you are eating or drinking or doing anything else, do all things for God's glory."—1 Corinthians 10:31.

23, 24. (a) What guidance does the Bible provide you on the use of alcoholic drinks? (Proverbs 23:20; 6:20; 1 Corinthians 6:9, 10) (b) How would you apply the counsel on this matter that is given at Romans 14:13-17, 21?

CHAPTER 15

Drugs—Key to Real Living?

LIKELY you have drugs—tranquilizers, "pep pills"—of some kind in your home, for today many of us live in a drug-obsessed society. For example, in the United States sales of the drug industry have increased more than thirtyfold since World War II. Dr. Mitchell S. Rosenthal said that in a recent year enough mood-altering drugs were prescribed by doctors "to keep every man, woman and child in [the United States] either 'up,' 'down' or 'out of it' for a solid month."

[2] Most drugs are prescribed for adults. But in some countries youths are consuming a big share of them 'to enjoy themselves.' They are also using other drugs that are not generally produced for medical use, including heroin, LSD and marijuana. Some youths may be inclined to reason: "If grown-ups take pills, use tobacco and get drunk, why shouldn't I enjoy myself smoking marijuana or taking drugs?" What do you think? Do you feel that drugs are a key to enjoying life more fully?

DRUGS TO WHICH MANY TURN

[3] There is a wide range of drugs that persons turn to for "kicks" or pleasure. You may already have heard much about them. But take a few moments to review what they are.

1, 2. (a) To what extent are drugs used among the folks that you know? (b) Why do young folks use drugs?
3-9. (a) What are the drugs that are used for "kicks" or pleasure? What effects do they have on the ones who use them? (b) Do you know of any experiences that people have had with drugs that verify these effects?

⁴ There are barbiturates, sometimes called "downers." They are sedatives, which doctors may prescribe to induce sleep. There are more than two dozen types of them, and over 525 *tons* (476 metric tons) are produced each year in the United States alone. A large part of the supply is diverted into illegal channels.

⁵ There are also many stimulants used, commonly known as "pep pills" or "uppers." Amphetamines are the principal ones. Some doctors prescribe them to suppress the appetite, reduce fatigue or relieve depression. However, it is estimated that half the legally manufactured amphetamines find their way into illegal channels.

⁶ LSD* is the most potent of the dozens of drugs that bring on hallucinations. In recent years many "underground" laboratories have begun making it. It produces weird effects in users. Vision is particularly altered. Illusions and hallucinations can occur even months after taking the last dose. On a "bad trip," what a person sees in visions may be terrifying.

⁷ Marijuana, a product of the cannabis plant, is one of the most widely used drugs. Do you know of persons who have smoked it? Its effect is milder than that of LSD, although it, too, produces a distortion of the senses. When one is smoking marijuana, five minutes may seem like an hour. Sound and colors may seem intensified.

⁸ Heroin is made from morphine, which comes from the opium poppy. It is a particularly dangerous drug. Persons may become addicted after injecting it only a few times, going through terrible withdrawal pains unless they get more.

---

* Lysergic acid diethylamide.

When people are addicted to heroin, it can destroy their will and capacity to learn. They become slaves to a habit that slowly destroys them. A New York congressman wrote: "Heroin has destroyed the functioning of our school system."

⁹ There are, of course, other drugs that many people think give them more out of life. Cocaine is one of these. Nicotine in tobacco is another. Should you use these drugs? As we have seen in the previous chapter, the Bible does not condemn moderate use of alcoholic beverages, which can relax a person and make his heart rejoice. Is it, then, proper or wise to use any of these many different drugs in an effort to make life more satisfying?

A PLACE FOR THEM?

¹⁰ Drugs evidently have their place, and a doctor may sometimes prescribe one for you because of a health problem. If you are in excruciating pain, a doctor might give you a shot of morphine to provide relief. Barbiturates and amphetamines have undoubtedly helped some patients with medical problems. Also, heroin is used in some places to relieve the suffering of terminally ill cancer patients.

¹¹ But, on the other hand, drugs are doing terrible harm to millions. About one million persons in the United States are reportedly barbiturate addicts, with over 3,000 dying each year from overdoses. Addiction to heroin not only results in many deaths a day due to overdoses but has turned tens of thousands into dangerous criminals. To support their expensive habits, addicts steal

10-12. (a) How might a doctor use a drug to help a person? (b) But how does abuse of drugs do terrible harm to people?

more than $3,000,000 in property in New York city, on the average, *every day!*

[12] What does this mean? Should drugs be abolished? Not necessarily, since many drugs can serve a good purpose. But the problem is the widespread *misuse* or *abuse* of them. Millions of persons use them where no treatment for illness is involved, and in large doses never intended in medical use. Often the user simply desires to get a dreamy feeling, or even to go into some sort of trance. Is such use justified?

EFFECT ON THE BODY

[13] You probably are aware that many drugs are available only on a doctor's prescription, and that some are even illegal in many countries. Ask yourself: Why? It is for the protection of all of us. Yes, drugs can be dangerous, even death-dealing. They are, in effect, a two-edged sword, capable, in some instances, of healing, but, in others, of hurting or even killing. *Drugs,* a book coauthored by a professor of pharmacology, explains:

[14] "All drugs are poisons, and all poisons are drugs. It is no accident that the words 'poison' and 'potion' come from the same root, or that the Greek word *pharmakon,* which we find rooted in our words 'pharmacy' and 'pharmacology,' originally meant both a healing draught and a deadly one."

[15] So, even when you are sick, taking a drug is a calculated risk. But because you value your life you may accept the risk and take a drug

13-17. (a) As shown in medical literature, what actually are all drugs? (b) So, why is their use even for medical purposes a calculated risk? (c) Analyze how the following scriptures indicate God's view of any use of drugs simply for pleasure or to "get high": 2 Corinthians 7:1; Romans 13:13; 12:1.

to relieve pain or to improve a poor condition of health. But would it be right for you to swallow, inject, smoke or sniff a drug in order to produce a so-called "high," to make you forget reality and go off into some dream world? Is this use of your marvelous, God-given body in harmony with what our Creator purposed?

16 Think about this. If you were able to give somebody an exquisite gift, say a brand-new automobile, how would you feel if he deliberately misused it? Say that he tried to operate it without ever putting oil into it or changing the oil, and he used it to deliver manure? You would probably be angry or disgusted with him for such stupid misuse of your gift, wouldn't you? How do you think, then, Jehovah God feels if we misuse our wonderful body, needlessly filling it with some poison in the quest of "kicks" or "thrills"? His Word lets us know by encouraging us: "Let us cleanse ourselves of every defilement of flesh and spirit, perfecting holiness in God's fear." (2 Corinthians 7:1) So, we cannot be living in harmony with God's will if, in a quest for "kicks" or "thrills," we take into our bodies a drug that defiles them.

17 Consider too this point. We have previously discussed what the Creator has advised about drunkenness. He plainly has shown in his Word that the person who loses control because of drinking too much debases himself, often becoming unclean and foolish, a source of embarrassment to persons around him. There is no question about it, our Maker rightly condemns drunkenness. So would God's view be different if a person lost self-control on heroin, marijuana or some other drug? Even though the reaction from

drugs is not exactly the same as from alcohol, one may lose control as much or even more so than do those who get drunk on alcohol. So from the wise and reasonable counsel found in the Bible, we can see the value of *not* turning to drugs for intoxicating thrills.

WHAT ABOUT USING TOBACCO?

[18] You may ask: "What, then, about the use of tobacco, which contains the harmful drug nicotine? Tens of millions of adults smoke, as they say, 'for pleasure.' Is this proper?" No, it is not, as evidenced by the warning that appears on cigarette packages sold in the United States: SMOKING IS DANGEROUS TO YOUR HEALTH. That fact is true no matter what country you live in. Why, then, do so many adults deliberately set a bad example for young people and, at the same time, ruin their own health by smoking? Mainly it is because they are addicted. A report in *Science World* explains:

[19] "The drug . . . that causes the addiction is *nicotine*. . . . When there is no nicotine, the body 'hungers' for it. So much so that the body sometimes becomes 'sick' without it. *Withdrawal symptoms*—a sick feeling—begin. . . . Some of these symptoms are drowsiness, headaches, stomach upsets, sweating, and irregular heart beats."

[20] Clearly, smoking abuses one's body; it is one of the 'defilements of the flesh' of which Christians are urged by our Creator to cleanse themselves. So you may feel that adults who smoke

18-21. (a) Why do so many people smoke tobacco, even though it is well known that doing so is dangerous to one's health? (b) Give at least two reasons why it would be wrong for a Christian to smoke.

are in a poor position to criticize young people who are abusing themselves with drugs. And it's true. If parents continue to abuse themselves by inhaling nicotine, how can they expect their children to take seriously what they say about the importance of avoiding drugs? Yet regardless of what others do or say, each of us individually is held accountable to God for his actions. And God's Word the Bible has something else to say that makes smoking wrong for a Christian.

[21] The Bible commands: "You must love your neighbor as yourself." (Matthew 22:39) But how can you smoke in the presence of others and still love your neighbor? We ask this in view of what the *Medical Tribune* explains: "Cigarette smoking is injurious not only to the smoker's health—it can be harmful to the innocent bystander as well." A prominent medical journal also noted: "Where the air circulation is typically poor, the non-smoker will be subjected to a significant health hazard from a smoker." Since smoking also harms

Just because millions of adults smoke, is this reason for you to do it?

those around a smoker, isn't it clear that you cannot smoke and truly love your neighbor?

IS MARIJUANA DIFFERENT?

[22] Some young people are inclined to compare smoking marijuana with drinking alcoholic beverages. They may see their parents or other adults "get high" on alcohol, and conclude that smoking marijuana to produce similar effects is no different. Is it?

[23] Recall that, whereas the Bible approves moderate use of alcoholic beverages, it condemns overindulgence, saying that "drunkards . . . will [not] inherit God's kingdom." (1 Corinthians 6:9, 10) However, many youths may say they use marijuana in moderation, and never to the extent to produce an effect similar to drunkenness. Yet marijuana is different from alcohol. Your body can convert alcohol into "fuel" that you can "burn" in your tissues. It is a food. But your body cannot use marijuana. Furthermore, alcohol is not retained for long periods of time in body or brain cells. It is dispersed from the body in a matter of hours. Marijuana's toxic substance, however, is not quickly passed off, and produces harmful effects on the body. Six doctors from Columbia University's College of Physicians and Surgeons, in a letter to the editor of the New York *Times,* explained:

> "Marijuana contains toxic substances . . . which are only soluble in fat and stored in body tissues, including brain, for weeks and months, like DDT. The storage capacity of tissues for these substances

22-25. (a) How is the effect of even moderate use of marijuana different from that of alcohol? (b) In warning us against harmful practices, how is God really helping us to get the best out of life? (Isaiah 48:17; Psalm 16:11; Proverbs 3:1-7)

is enormous—which explains their slow deleterious effects in habitual smokers. Anyone using these substances more than once a week cannot be drug free."

[24] Thus Tulane University's Dr. Robert Heath brands the comparison between alcohol and marijuana as "ridiculous." He states that alcohol has "a temporary effect. Marijuana is complex with a persisting effect." Evidently even the moderate, regular use of marijuana can have bad effects, as the Detroit *Free Press* notes: "Medical researchers are reporting new discoveries which indicate that marijuana—and its big brother [hashish]—are indeed dangerous to physical and mental health when used regularly, even once or twice a week."

[25] Truly, we can be thankful for the guiding principles our Creator has given us. He loves us, and for that reason urges us to avoid what will defile our bodies and thereby hurt us, rather than contribute to our lasting happiness and welfare. Certain drugs may be able to benefit a person who is sick, but they can only harm those who turn to them in the quest for pleasure. They are *not* the key to real living.

CHAPTER 16

Sports and Entertainment

THERE is a worldwide interest in various sports and forms of entertainment. Each year *billions* of dollars are spent on enjoying them. Do you share an interest in these things? Do you, for example, like to go skiing or boating? Do you enjoy swimming, playing tennis or participating in other sports? Or do you perhaps find pleasure in going to movies or watching television programs?

² Some persons would say that such pleasures are wrong. What do you think? Why, some persons even claim that the Bible disapproves of these things. But, frankly, such persons have misrepresented the Bible and its author, Jehovah God. God's Word speaks favorably of young people deriving pleasure from recreational activities. For example, in describing God's blessed people, the Bible says: "The public squares of the city themselves will be filled with boys and girls playing." Also, it says that there is "a time for dancing." (Zechariah 8:5; Ecclesiastes 3:4, *New English Bible*) Obviously, God purposed that we should gain pleasure from wholesome recreational activities. One of the fruits of God's spirit is "joy." (Galatians 5:22) And our enjoyment of healthful recreational activities is normal and natural.

1, 2. (a) What sports or other entertainment do you particularly enjoy? (b) What is there about Jehovah's handiwork that indicates that he wants us to enjoy life? (Psalm 104:14-24)

GUIDANCE TO ENHANCE PLEASURE

[3] To help us to gain pleasure from such activities, God has lovingly provided us with guidance. For example, so that we would avoid the unhealthful results of overeating, God's Word counsels: "Do not come to be among . . . those who are gluttonous eaters of flesh." (Proverbs 23:20) Similarly, he gives us this wise counsel in connection with recreational activities: "Be training yourself with godly devotion as your

3-8. (a) What balanced counsel on recreation is found at 1 Timothy 4:7, 8? (b) How is "bodily training" beneficial? But what can happen when a person becomes too serious about sports? (c) What problems can confront a person if he gets involved in playing on a school team? What should help him to decide wisely as to whether this is what he will do?

aim. For bodily training is beneficial for a little; but godly devotion is beneficial for all things, as it holds promise of the life now and that which is to come."—1 Timothy 4:7, 8.

⁴ So the Bible shows that "bodily training," such as we get in sports, has its place. It is good for us; it can help us to develop physical co-ordination, flexibility, muscle tone and strength. Also, it can refresh us mentally, especially if we spend a lot of time studying. But note that the Bible cautions that "bodily training is beneficial for a little." What can happen if such Bible advice is ignored and you become totally absorbed in sports?

⁵ For one thing, it can spoil the fun, making sports "serious business" rather than a welcome recreation. Pointing to the effects of overstressing competitive games, sports psychologist Bruce Ogilvie said: "I once interviewed the rookies in 10 major league baseball camps and 87 per cent of them said they wished they'd never played Little League baseball because it took the joy out of what had been a fun game."

⁶ Also, some sports, such as football, can be dangerous, especially when your body is in the process of developing physically. *Science Digest* reports that about 12,000,000 American children, before they turn eighteen, suffer some *permanent* physical impairment from engaging in sports! One of professional football's most prominent players would not let his two sons play in the children's football leagues. "Parents don't stop to think of all the things that can go wrong for a young fellow," he said. "For one thing, he can come home with a handful of teeth." What has

made some sports so dangerous is the extreme competitiveness—the win-at-all-costs attitude—that is often encouraged.

⁷ Another thing to consider is the associations to which playing organized sports may expose you. Locker-room talk generally has the reputation of being sexually immoral. Furthermore, when a team takes a trip to play another school, one may for an extended time be in the company of persons who have little regard for faithfulness to God. This is something to think about, since God's Word stresses "training yourself with *godly devotion as your aim.*" And how practical would it be to get involved in something that could easily damage your moral principles and your relationship with your Creator?

⁸ So sports are much like other things that are good when they are kept in balance—when they don't dominate your life so as to overshadow more important things, or expose you to damaging situations. How exhilarating it can be to play a fast-moving sport and experience the thrill as one's body responds and performs feats of skill! It can provide a joy and satisfaction that is long remembered. And it can help you to appreciate our grand Creator who made us with the capabilities to do such things.

MOVIES AND TELEVISION

⁹ The type of movie and TV entertainment we choose can also affect our relationship with God. Some movies and TV shows are delightful enter-

----

9-14. (a) When selecting a movie or TV show to watch, against what sort of thing does one need to be on guard? (b) How would it affect a person if he watched as entertainment things that are morally corrupt? Why? Even though we know that such acts are wrong, why should we not underestimate the effect that watching them could have on us?

tainment; some may even enhance our appreciation of our Creator's marvelous handiwork. But no doubt you have noticed that many shows have exploded with stories featuring adultery, fornication, lesbianism, homosexuality, violence and mass killing. These may be viewed as entertainment. But how do they affect a person?

[10] Well, ask yourself: How have you become the person you are today? Is it not by your environment and education, by what you have been taking into your mind, especially through your eyes and ears? Yes, to a large extent *you are what you feed your mind*. The more you are exposed to a certain thing, the more likely it becomes part of you.

[11] You wouldn't think of choosing to eat a meal of filthy garbage, would you? What, then, if you are continually exposed to mental garbage? It is bound to become part of your thinking. When watching a motion picture, you are, in effect, associating with the kinds of persons being portrayed on the screen. And movies are deliberately designed to involve you emotionally with the characters, often arousing sympathy for the wrongdoer—the fornicator, the homosexual, even the murderer. Do you want to get deeply involved in such a way with homosexuals, lesbians, fornicators, adulterers and criminals?

[12] Still, as you watch some act of sexual immorality or violence on the screen, you may think: "Why, I'd never do a thing like that!" True, right now it might repel you if someone were to suggest that you steal from your neighbor, lie to your friends or commit fornication. But what if you were to keep company with thieves, fornicators and homosexuals long enough, listening to their distorted thinking? In time, you might well be-

Does what you watch have any effect on you?

come sympathetic toward them. What at first seemed repulsive might not seem that way in time. And consider this: How did the majority of homosexuals get to be that way? By spending time thinking about it and by associating with others who were that way.

[13] You may feel that you would not engage in immorality. But what if you go to motion pictures with persons of the opposite sex and watch repeated acts of necking, petting and immorality? What will you be more likely to do after such movies, especially if you also have access to alcoholic beverages, which lower inhibitions? You know the answer. In effect, many of today's films shout out: "We're going to engage in badness! We're going to break all laws, even God's!" Is that the kind of influence you want working on you?

[14] Do you honestly think that you are above being corrupted by bad influences? Remember, millions of once-decent, hardworking Europeans were "brainwashed" by Nazi propaganda to commit or support terrible crimes against humanity. So do not underestimate the effect that the corrupt propaganda spread through motion pictures on sex and violence can have on you.

FILLING THE NEED FOR RECREATION

[15] Our Creator made us with a need for recreation. But he never purposed that it should center around moral filth or violence, around the breaking of his laws. True, if you exclude movies and TV shows that feature these things, you may find that you are excluding a great many films and television programs. But there are still many wholesome forms of recreation that you can enjoy.

[16] After all, what good is recreation or entertainment if, after it's finished, you don't feel refreshed or if it leaves you feeling disturbed or upset—as the saying goes, with a 'bad taste in your mouth'? If someone offered you something to eat and it looked good and tasted nice but after eating it you felt sick, would you go back for 'seconds'? Be selective, then, as to how you spend your free time in recreation and entertainment. Don't just "kill time" by settling for any kind of entertainment that happens to be on hand, but put some life into that free time by doing something that will bring real enjoyment and refreshment, something that you can look back on and remember with pleasure.

15-19. What are some wholesome activities in which we can satisfy our need for recreation?

[17] There is a variety of outdoor sports that you can play. Many folks have had hours of enjoyment hiking in the woods, playing handball and badminton, or pitching horseshoes. Some have set up a Ping-Pong table or pool table at home and invited their friends over to play such games. If you check with your parents, you may find that they will welcome your doing this.

[18] You may also be able to visit museums or other places of interest that both entertain and inform. Have you visited a chicken farm, a dairy, an auction or a printing plant? If you live in a city, there may be government departments that can give you facts about places of interest in the city. They may tell you about the industries in your vicinity that welcome visitors. In addition, trips to scenic spots such as lakes, mountains and beaches can be delightful recreation, especially when families can enjoy these things together.

[19] Of course, there is the need to exercise caution so that these pleasurable pursuits don't become the chief objective in our lives, and we thereby fail to receive the benefits that they can provide. Yet how grateful we can be that our Creator has made us with the capacity to share in and enjoy such a wide variety of recreational activities! These can indeed make life more worth while.

CHAPTER 17

The Music and Dancing You Choose

MAN'S Creator built music into human surroundings. Not just the clear, flowing tones that spring from the throats of birds, but the gurgle of brooks, the whisper of the wind in the trees, the chirp of crickets, the croak of frogs and the calls of many others of earth's creatures— all of these have a musical sound to them. Not surprisingly, then, the development of musical instruments dates all the way back to the dawn of human history.

² Dancing, too, has an ancient history. In Israel, Moses' sister Miriam led the women "with tambourines and in dances." Also, after God helped King David defeat depraved enemies "the women began coming out from all the cities

Dancing has a long history

of Israel with song and dances." It is evident, too, that Jesus Christ approved of dancing, since he

1-3. (a) In what way is it true that the Creator has built music into our natural surroundings? (b) Give examples to show that the Bible speaks with approval of dancing.

mentioned it as a part of a proper celebration in his illustration about the prodigal son. Jesus spoke of "a music concert and dancing" being arranged when the prodigal returned. The Bible shows that some dancing was by individuals or by groups of men, or of women.—Exodus 15:20; 1 Samuel 18:6; Luke 15:25.

³ Does that mean that all music and dancing are necessarily good? Or do you need to be selective in the music you listen to and the dances in which you might engage? What can help us to determine? How much does it really matter?

CHOICE IN DANCING

⁴ There is a wide variety of dances—from graceful waltzes to lively polkas. There are Latin-American congas, rumbas and sambas, also merengues, beguines and bossa novas, many of these having an African background. There is also rock 'n' roll, as well as more recent dances. Is there good reason why you might have objection to certain of these dances?

⁵ There is if the dance arouses you sexually and brings a temptation to commit sexual immorality. It could cause you many problems.

⁶ Ancient fertility dances, for example, were designed to incite sexual passions, and certain modern dances have been reminiscent of these. Some years ago *Time* magazine observed:

"The Twist at first was an innocent enough dance . . . But the youngsters at [a certain New York nightclub] have revived The Twist and parodied it into a replica of some ancient tribal puberty rite."

4-6. (a) What could make some dances objectionable for Christians? (Colossians 3:5, 6) (b) Why have certain modern dances been compared to ancient fertility dances?

⁷ Many dances in recent years have been variants of the Twist. The dancers do not touch, but the hips and shoulders may gyrate in sexually suggestive ways. A young person's passions may easily be aroused by watching a body perform these gyrations. A girl, for example, may not think anything about it, simply being caught up in the movements of the dance. But she shouldn't ignore the effect on onlookers, and on what they might think of her, as this letter to the editor of the New York *Times Magazine* observes: "Let's hope that the young (and not so young) bodies of our Twisters are lying, that their minds do not behave inside the way their pelvises and pectorals do outside."

⁸ Even though you have no wrong motive, if you participate in such dances you would be wise to consider the kind of attraction you may be to other young persons. For example, are they attracted to you on the basis of the sexual arousal they get from you, a type of arousal they can get from persons who dress in tight clothing, and gyrate their hips and make various erotic gestures? Do you want to attract someone simply on that basis? Or do you want the kind of person who likes you for what you are? for the things that you feel are important in life? for your conversation? Are you interested in someone who takes pleasure in doing things for you, or only in what he can get from you?

⁹ Even ballroom dancing, which emphasizes foot patterns accompanied by graceful movements of the body and in which partners hold one an-

---

7-10. (a) If a person shared in such dancing, on what basis might others be attracted to the individual? Would you want to attract persons of the opposite sex on that basis? (b) Even in ballroom dancing, why is caution needed?

other, may sometimes be sexually stimulating due to close physical contact. So, if you participate in such dances, considerately recognize the possibility that your partner could be stimulated improperly even though you may feel that it is not close enough for you to develop sensual pleasure from the dancing.

[10] It's a fact that most dances cannot be classified as either proper or improper. Many of them can be done either in a decent, proper way, or in a way that violates the counsel of God's Word to behave in a clean, wholesome manner.

CHOICE OF MUSIC

[11] Just as with dancing, care and thought are also necessary in your choice of the music you listen to. Why? Because music has power. And, like any other power, it can serve for good or for harm.

[12] Where does music's power come from? From its ability to cause a certain feeling, mood or spirit in people. Music can relax and soothe, or refresh and enliven. You can almost "feel" the difference between a vigorous march and a soft serenade. Music can stir every human emotion— love, tenderness, reverence, sadness, anger, hatred and passion. Throughout history men have recognized music's power and have used it to move people in certain ways. For instance, part of the triumph of the French Revolution is frequently credited to what one writer calls "the blood-curdling call to arms" of the song La Marseillaise. And schools often have their "fight songs" used before athletic contests.

11, 12. How does music exercise power? Cite examples.

[13] In the Bible the heart is closely associated with emotions and motivation, so God's Word counsels: "More than all else that is to be guarded, safeguard your heart, for out of it are the sources of life." (Proverbs 4:23) Since music's emotional power is a fact, our guarding our hearts requires being selective about the music we choose.

[14] True, music's moving effect is only temporary. But it is often long enough to give a decided push in a certain direction, or to lower resistance to a certain attraction or temptation. If you studied chemistry in school you learned about "catalysts." You learned that the combining of two or more chemicals can often be achieved only by using some other ingredient that, in effect, brings the chemicals together. That ingredient is a "catalyst." Now, we all have certain weaknesses and wrong inclinations, and so we feel tempted at times to do certain things that are wrong. Suppose circumstances come up that encourage you to do a wrong act. Music can be the "catalyst" that will cause desire and circumstances to combine— resulting in something you may afterward seriously regret. On the basis of her studies, one researcher for a government commission studying pornography said:

[15] "Music, by playing on girls' emotions to arouse love and affection, frequently serves as a catalyst for love and thereby a stimulus for sexual arousal in the adolescent female. . . . The music surfaces this feeling."

[16] Yes, the impulse that music supplies, though temporary, may be all that is needed to trigger you into a course or way of life that is itself

---

13-16. (a) How is the counsel at Proverbs 4:23 related to one's choice of music? (b) How can music be a "catalyst," and sometimes with lastingly harmful results?

long lasting or that produces results that are. So, is it not worth your while to use discernment where music is involved?

THE PROBLEM OF DECIDING

[17] Actually, no one can provide you with a list that immediately identifies what music is good and what is bad. The reason is that among practically all kinds of music there is none that can be stamped as "all good" or "all bad." You have to use your mind and heart for discerning the individual value of certain music, and be guided by principles such as those already considered. And your choice tells others something as to the kind of person you are.

[18] "Does not the ear itself test out words as

17, 18. By listening to a piece of music, how can you determine whether it is something that is good for you or something that is bad?

the palate tastes food?" asked Job long ago. (Job 12:11) So, too, your ear can test out music. Even without the words, you can often tell what kind of mood or spirit a piece is designed to produce, what kind of conduct it encourages. That was the case with the music that Moses heard on coming down from Mount Sinai and approaching the Israelite camp. As he said to Joshua: "It is not the sound of the singing over mighty performance [a victory song], and it is not the sound of the singing of defeat [a mournful singing]; it is the sound of other singing that I am hearing." The singing actually reflected wild and idolatrous immoral activity.—Exodus 32:15-19, 25.

[19] Consider more recent examples. Classical music, for instance, generally has a dignified, sometimes majestic sound. But while much of it may have a rather noble effect on one's thoughts, some of it deals with and even glorifies the sordid or selfish side of life. It is worth remembering that many famous classical composers lived immoral, even dissolute, lives. And though they generally wrote for an audience that supposedly appreciated the "finer things of life," it is almost unavoidable that some of their warped outlook and warped emotions would show up in some of their music, with or without words. So, if we want to guard the health of our minds and hearts, even so-called "serious" music cannot be accepted without question.

[20] At the other end of the musical spectrum from classical compositions we find the syncopated jazz and rock music. Even here one finds some

19-22. (a) Against what do those who like classical music need to be on guard? (b) As to the effect of some jazz and rock music, what facts deserve thoughtful consideration?

music that is melodic and moderate. But some of it is wild and strident. That is why musicians themselves distinguish between jazz and rock music that is "soft" and that which is "hot," "hard" or "acid." You should be able to tell what kind of conduct the music is promoting—your ear, your mind and heart should tell you. The words or the tone of certain music is sometimes so obvious that people easily associate it with certain types of conduct or kinds of persons. The Bible, for example, speaks of the "songs of drinkers" and the "song of a prostitute." (Psalm 69:12; Isaiah 23:15, 16) What about today?

²¹ If, for example, you read in the newspaper about a music concert or festival and the report tells of people screaming, girls fainting, the use of drugs and of the police having to be brought in to keep the theater from being wrecked—what kind of music would you think was involved in the performance? If you hear of a popular young singer or musician dying of an overdose of drugs —what kind of music would you think he or she specialized in?

²² You probably know that many young people are drawn to rock music because they believe that its lyrics describe the realities and problems of the world around them. Perhaps more than any other form of popular music, rock music tries to put across a message: on the problems of growing up, the generation gap, drugs, sex, civil rights, dissent, poverty, war and similar topics. It tries to express many young people's discontent with social injustices and their ideas for a better world. But what has been the general effect? What has it done for most young people? What real solutions have its philosophies brought

them? If such music is designed to bring realities into focus, why is so much of it drug-oriented, some lyrics being understandable only to those who take drugs? These are questions to consider.

[23] So, your choice of music is no light matter. You can let others decide for you simply by going along with the crowd, choosing what is popular, what has mass appeal. Or you can think for yourself and use care in selecting, guided by the enduring and superior wisdom found in God's Word. Ecclesiastes 7:5 says: "Better is it to hear the rebuke of someone wise than to be the man hearing the song of the stupid ones." The "stupidity" the Bible talks about is no mere mental dumbness but means moral stupidity, following a course that can only bring future trouble.

[24] You may feel that you can listen to music containing some words that go contrary to what is true and right or that has a sensual, wild sound to it, and still not be affected. You may feel similarly about the dances you dance. But what kind of influence are you on others? Do you feel as the apostle Paul, who said that he was willing to forgo even such proper things as eating meat if thereby he could avoid becoming a stumbling block to others? With what kind of persons does the music you choose identify you?

[25] Your choice, then, of the music to which you listen and the dances in which you might engage shows whether you are simply interested in a "good time" or in a *good life,* an everlasting one in God's favor.

23-25. (a) In connection with music, what is the point of the counsel at Ecclesiastes 7:5? (b) Whom should we consider when choosing music and dances? Why? (1 Corinthians 10:31-33; Philippians 1:9, 10) (c) So why is our choice as to music and dancing no light matter?

CHAPTER 18

Does Sexual Morality Make Sense?

T HE pressure to engage in premarital sex today is powerful in many places. The world,
in fact, is caught up in a "sexual revolution." The
New York *Daily News* explains: "Sexual relationships without marriage are now broadly recognized by parents, colleges and the public generally. There is a sort of quiet tolerance of
immorality, as if it would be futile to stem a
new irresistible tide."

[2] Many people demand freedom to have sexual
relations with whomever they wish and in any
way that they choose. Such attitudes cause uncertainty for many individuals. A college girl tells
of a typical problem she encountered on a date:
"He would say, Why not? I would spend half the
date trying to explain to him what was so special
about morality. Then afterward I would ask myself, Why not?" Might you, too, have wondered,
"Why not?" Does sexual morality really make
sense?

[3] Youths commonly believe that, since they are
physically capable of having sexual intercourse,
and since it reportedly is 'a lot of fun,' this is
something for them to do. But is it really? Is
sex prior to marriage proper? Does it help to
make life worth living?

1-3. How do many people in the world feel about premarital
sex?

GOOD EFFECTS OR BAD?

[4] What about the claim of some that sexual freedom brings greater personal happiness, that it's 'a lot of fun'? *The Journal of the American Medical Association* reported this conclusion of a youth who had premarital sex relations with many girls: "I have learned that this did not bring me happiness." Girls are even less likely to realize happiness from premarital relations. A tearful young college student said of such an experience: "It sure wasn't worth it—it was no fun at the time, and I've been worried ever since."

[5] Such worry often is justified for a number of reasons. Pointing to one reason, a health official said that gonorrhea threatened to infect 50 percent of United States teen-agers in just five years! And medical authorities say that modern drugs are proving ineffective in stopping the growth of both gonorrhea and syphilis, the major venereal diseases. All too often those affected realize it too late to avoid serious and irreversible damage to their bodies. Does it make sense to risk the chance of suffering permanent damage, perhaps even blindness or sterility, as a result of immorality?

[6] Also, there exists the strong possibility of becoming pregnant. Millions of unmarried girls do. Many of these go through the dangers and emotional strains of abortions. Others are forced into unhappy marriages. Still others face a long, unhappy struggle to rear an illegitimate child. So

---

4-7. (a) What are some of the common results from engaging in premarital sex? (b) What shows that loose sex practices are not really a "new" morality? (Judges 19:22-25; Jude 7) (c) Why is the counsel at 1 Corinthians 6:18 such a serious matter? (Acts 15:28, 29; 1 Thessalonians 4:3, 7, 8)

it is easy to see that, although contraceptives are becoming more easily available to teen-agers, they don't give "guaranteed" freedom from pregnancy.

[7] Really, there is nothing new or "modern" about sexual looseness. It has been around for a long, long time. The people of Sodom and Gomorrah practiced it nearly two thousand years before the birth of Jesus Christ. If you read the history of the old Roman Empire you will see that it was notable for sexual looseness of all the kinds carried on today. In fact, its fall came largely because of moral decay. Surely, it is a wise thing to heed the Bible's command to "flee from fornication."—1 Corinthians 6:18.

MORALITY A SIGN OF WEAKNESS?

[8] However, you may be challenged to commit fornication and, if you refuse, others may accuse you of being weak. In some places fornication has become an accepted practice. Two doctors writing in *Medical Aspects of Human Sexuality* observe: "Young people have come to feel guilty for refusing to have ready sex, and there are instances where young women have expressed shame at still being virgins at the age of 25." Is it a sign of weakness to refuse to enter sexual relations before marriage? Well, which would you say takes more strength—to give in to passion or to contain it?

[9] Actually, any weakling can give in to the sex urge. But it takes a real "man" (or a real "woman") to control that urge until taking a

8-11. (a) Why does refraining from premarital sex call for moral strength? (b) As related at Proverbs chapter 7, what shows that the young man who got immorally involved lacked good motive? (c) How is the firmness for right principles on the part of a young woman of Shunem illustrated?

mate in marriage. It takes even more strength now when the global trend is going the other way, because it means bucking the current.

[10] The Bible book of Proverbs presents an account illustrating this point. It relates the way a young man from among the "inexperienced ones," lacking in good heart motive, wanders down into a street where he is approached by a prostitute. Under the pressure of her shrewd persuasiveness, he caves in and "all of a sudden he is going after her, like a bull that comes even to the slaughter, and just as if fettered [or shackled] for the discipline of a foolish man." (Proverbs 7:6-23) He did not have the moral strength to resist.

[11] But earlier in this publication we read about the attractive young maiden of Shunem who resisted all the enticements that wealthy King Solomon could offer, preferring to remain true to the young shepherd she hoped to marry. Yes, instead of being like a "door" that could easily be swung open, she proved to her older brothers that she was as firm as a "wall" in her determination to keep her virginity for the man she was waiting for.—Song of Solomon 8:8-10.

WHY SEXUAL MORALITY MAKES SENSE

[12] The main reason sexual morality makes sense is that it is the way set out by the One who knows the most about human happiness: Jehovah God. Think about it. Jehovah God has lovingly made provision for the transmission of

12-14. (a) Why does it make good sense to conform to God's rules regarding sex? (b) What do Hebrews 13:4 and 1 Corinthians 6:9, 10 say that the future holds for fornicators? What is meant by fornication?

human life by means of sex relations, and this is a very wonderful and sacred thing. We have all received of its benefits, because we are living. If we accept its benefits, doesn't this place an obligation on us to accept God's regulation of the entire process? Surely, as our Life-Giver, Jehovah God has the right to set forth rules of conduct as to the use of our procreative organs with the life-transmitting powers.

[13] Through the apostle Paul, God tells us: "Let marriage be honorable among all, and the marriage bed be without defilement, for God will judge fornicators and adulterers." (Hebrews 13:4) Fornication includes not only promiscuous sex relations with just anyone—it also includes premarital sex, as between persons who are engaged but not yet married.

[14] God's Word is very definite in condemning fornication and other loose conduct. It says that persons practicing such things will have no part in God's kingdom. The Bible says: "Do not be misled. Neither fornicators, nor idolaters, nor adulterers, nor men kept for unnatural purposes, nor men who lie with men, nor thieves, nor greedy persons, nor drunkards, nor revilers, nor extortioners will inherit God's kingdom."—1 Corinthians 6:9, 10.

[15] This positiveness of God's law is really for our good. The sexual urges can be very strong, and occasions come in the life of most persons when it would be easy to give in under the pressure of temptation. If God's law on the matter were vague or weak, it certainly would not help

---

15-19. (a) Why should we actually hate sexual immorality? (Psalm 97:10) (b) What can help us to cultivate such proper hatred?

us much in those times. But because it is so clear and forceful it helps us to keep our senses, bolsters our moral courage and, most important, it helps us to learn to hate the wrong course. Do you actually hate the course of sexual immorality? Why should you?

¹⁶ If that course at times seems appealing, ask yourself: 'Would I want those of my own family to engage in it, my parents or my brothers and sisters? Would I want them to have illegitimate children? Would this increase my love and respect for them?' If not, then isn't that course worth hating? Surely you would not want to make yourself like a public towel on which any man or woman can wipe his or her hands by means of immorality.

¹⁷ What of children born from such an immoral course? Suppose you, if a girl, gave birth to such a child—who would care for it? Your mother and father? You yourself? How would you do it? And how would the child feel when it grows up and finds out how it was conceived? Or if you refused to shoulder the responsibility and you put the child up for adoption, how would other people feel about you? How would you feel about yourself? You might try to cover up the birth, then put the child out of sight by giving it up for adoption and thus try to run

away from shame and responsibility. But you can never run away from yourself, can you?

¹⁸ If you, as a male, fathered an illegitimate child, would your conscience be at rest? Think of all the trouble and shame brought on the mother as well as your child. Certainly that is something to avoid.

¹⁹ Really, what good has ever come from the course of sexual immorality? Why is it that so many undesirable things are associated with it, including crippling venereal diseases, abortions, jealous fights and even murders? Why is it that in lands where great sexual "freedom" is allowed, the divorce rates are often among the highest in the world? Does divorce spell success or is it evidence of failure? Is it a sign of true happiness or of unhappiness and dissatisfaction?

²⁰ On the other hand, sexual morality does make sense because those who hold to it have a far better likelihood of a successful marriage. This is because they have kept marriage in high regard, respecting God's arrangement and respecting their future mates and their mutual right to receive a clean partner in marriage.

²¹ In fact, the more careful you are to avoid loose conduct or the taking of liberties during courtship and engagement periods, the more likely will be your success in marriage. Then neither you nor your mate will have nagging doubts of the genuineness of the other's love due to suspicion that sex was the sole motive for marrying. For marriage, after all, is not just a union of two bodies—it is a union of two *persons*. And there must be mutual high regard and love for the

20, 21. How can avoiding sexual immorality improve your prospects for a successful marriage?

person if the marriage is to bring lasting happiness.

MAKING A WISE CHOICE

²² Love based solely on passion is not an enduring love. It is a selfish, greedy love. That kind of love is well illustrated in the Bible by the case of one of David's sons, named Amnon. He "fell in love" with his beautiful half sister Tamar. Then, through trickery, he forced her into having relations with him. After that, what? The record tells us: "And Amnon began hating her with a very great hatred, because the hatred with which he hated her was greater than the love with which he had loved her." He sent her out into the street. (2 Samuel 13:1-19) Now, if you are a young woman, should you naïvely think that, because some boy expresses passionate love for you and wants you to have relations with him, this means he sincerely loves you? He may very well turn out to be just as Amnon was.

²³ The Bible tells us that the wife of Egyptian officer Potiphar expressed the same kind of interest in young Joseph, who served in their house. When he resisted all her attempts to seduce him, she then showed her true colors. She viciously lied to her husband about Joseph, causing him to be unjustly imprisoned.—Genesis 39:7-20.

²⁴ Yes, so-called sexual "freedom" changes what should be pleasurable and clean into something cheap and detestable. So, which do you want—an occasional brief moment of illicit sexual excite-

22-24. (a) What helpful lesson can a young woman learn from the Bible account about Amnon and Tamar? (b) What shows that the passion displayed by Potiphar's wife was not enduring love?

ment with all the risks and problems it involves, or the satisfaction of having a clean conscience before God and all persons, with self-respect, day in and day out?

[25] If you want to stay free from immorality, then stay free from the things that lead to it: conversation that always dwells on the opposite sex, also reading material or pictures that have only one aim—to excite sexual passion. Keep your mind, your eyes and your tongue occupied with clean, positive things, working toward worthwhile goals that bring enduring benefits and that leave no shame or heartache.

[26] Above all, strengthen your knowledge and appreciation of your Creator and of the rightness and wisdom of his ways. Look to him in prayer and fix your heart on the things he promises to those who serve him. You can hold firmly to the course of sexual morality if you really want to, for Jehovah God and his Son will give you the strength you need to do it.

25, 26. What things will help us to avoid getting involved in sexual immorality? (Ephesians 5:3, 4; Philippians 4:8)

CHAPTER 19

Dating and Courtship

EVERY normal person wants to get real enjoyment out of life. The Bible shows that this is proper, listing joy as one of the "fruits" of God's spirit. (Galatians 5:22) Many young people, especially in Western lands, look to dating as a prime means of finding enjoyment. They often arrange to spend time, unchaperoned, with someone of the opposite sex. What can be said about this?

² You may assume dating to be a normal, expected practice, since it is so common in many places. Yet it hasn't always been, as the book *The Family in Social Context* explains: "Dating as we know it probably emerged after World War I." In many countries, however, dating never has become the custom. In fact, the prospective bride and groom may still not meet until their wedding day. The arrangements for their marriage are carried out by their respective parents, or perhaps by a "matchmaker" or "go-between."

³ Of course, if you live where dating and courtship are accepted as normal, the absence of these customs in certain lands may seem hard to understand. But people living in those lands may be equally puzzled by the customs where you live. They may view dating and courtship as unwise,

---

1-4. (a) How recently did dating become a common practice? (b) Where dating is not customary, how may marriages be arranged? (c) In the final analysis, what determines how good or how bad these customs are?

or even somewhat offensive. A girl from India explained to a well-known Western marriage counselor: "How would we be able to judge the character of a boy we met and got friendly with? We are young and inexperienced. Our parents are older and wiser, and they aren't as easily deceived as we would be. . . . It's so important that the man I marry should be the right one. I could so easily make a mistake if I had to find him for myself."

⁴ So, rather than taking a narrow-minded viewpoint and thinking that the only way to do things is the way people in your own locality do them, it is good to broaden out your thinking. After all, in the final analysis, it is the way things

work out, the results, that determine how good or how bad certain customs are. In the Bible at Ecclesiastes 7:8, we read: "Better is the end afterward of a matter than its beginning." And we must admit that in many countries where dating and courtship are the custom, a large percentage of marriages are not working out well but are ending in divorce.

WHAT, THEN, ABOUT DATING?

[5] If you believe in reasoning things out, you will want to consider not just the short-range effects of dating but also the longer-range results. Our Creator helps us to look at matters from this long-range viewpoint. He wants for us what will bring us true and lasting happiness. So he urges in his Word: "Rejoice, young man, in your youth, and let your heart do you good in the days of your young manhood, and walk in the ways of your heart and in the things seen by your eyes. But know that on account of all these the true God will bring you into judgment. So remove vexation from your heart, and ward off calamity from your flesh; for youth and the prime of life are vanity." (Ecclesiastes 11:9, 10) What does this mean?

[6] It means that the Creator wants you to enjoy your youth, but, at the same time, not to engage in conduct that will adversely affect your life later on. Unfortunately this so often occurs, even as a writer of modern times observed: "The greatest part of mankind employ their first years to make their last miserable." You don't want that to happen to you, do you? Neither does God want it to occur. Yet the Bible is also showing here in Ecclesiastes that God holds young persons responsible for what they do. Their youth will not excuse them from facing the consequences of the course they choose.

[7] This all bears directly on the matter of dating. How so? Well, ask yourself: "Why do I want to date? What am I looking for that I couldn't

5-8. (a) How does what is said at Ecclesiastes 11:9, 10 help us to take a long-range view of our conduct? (b) Why do many young people want to date?

enjoy, for example, as part of a group? Why do I want to pair off with a person of the opposite sex?" Isn't the basic reason the growing attraction you feel toward those of the opposite sex? This can be seen from the fact that physical attractiveness usually has a lot to do with one's being desirable as a "date."

[8] Many young persons who date are not seriously thinking of marriage at present, or that they necessarily would like the person they date for a marriage partner. In most places where dating is considered to be customary, it is viewed merely as a form of recreation, a way to spend an evening or a weekend. And some persons, not wanting to be viewed as "different," date because others their own age do. Yet, there is no question that dating can lead to "vexation," and even "calamity." Let's consider why it can.

THE EFFECTS OF PHYSICAL CONTACT

[9] More often than not, dating involves some physical contact—holding hands, kissing, or something beyond that. At first, just touching the other person's hand may be very pleasurable, causing one to feel a warm glow. But after a while it may lose its thrill and may not have the same effect. Something more, such as kissing, may appeal. But, then, that too may become ordinary, even a little stale. Why is this?

[10] Because where sexual passion is involved it is all part of a chain of events designed to lead to a specific outcome. The first link is the first

9-11. (a) What physical contact is usually involved in dating? Why is there the natural inclination to become progressively more intimate? (b) Why may this result in nervous tension for an unmarried person? (c) If the physical contact leads to fornication, how can that result in calamity of many kinds?

touch. The last link is sexual relations, which God's Word shows is reserved for marriage mates. Everything in between can lead up to that last link of the chain. So, then, if you are not married, is it wise to start with the first link, or any of the others? To do so is likely to bring "vexation." Why? Because your body is going to get itself ready for something it should not receive now, that last link. Stimulating the desire for sexual relations but not fulfilling this desire may lead to frustration and nervous tension.

[11] Fornication will not end the "vexation." Rather, it can lead to "calamity." How? In a number of ways. It can result in venereal disease. The girl could become pregnant, and this could pressure a couple into a marriage they really are not prepared for, adversely affecting their future happiness. Or the young man may refuse to marry the young woman, and she is then obliged to bring up the child herself with no husband. Or she may be tempted to undergo an abortion, which the Bible shows to be a form of murder. Is this not "calamity"? You may be determined that dating will not have these consequences for you. But many who were just as determined as you are have wound up facing these troubles. Really, then, the question comes back to whether you are ready for marriage or not.

YOUR PERSONAL DEVELOPMENT

[12] Even when dating doesn't lead directly to "calamity," it can have other disadvantages. One is the way it tends to narrow your interest down so soon to just one person. This is at a time when,

12, 13. How can dating hinder one's development? So, what kind of relationships can be more beneficial?

for the development of your own emotional maturity, you can benefit most from association with a wide variety of persons. If you are in your young manhood, why not first concentrate on becoming a real man by having your main friendships with other men who demonstrate regard for what is right? You can learn manly abilities and ways from them. If you are in your young womanhood, why not interest yourself first in developing into a true woman, benefiting from association with those who are and who can help you to develop fine womanly abilities and ways? Dating really interrupts and slows down such development.

[13] Before dating became a popular custom, young people found plenty of things to bring them enjoyment. You can too. You can find real enjoyment in conversing, learning, developing skills, working on projects, playing games, going places and seeing things. And you can find great pleasure in doing these things with someone of your own sex or with a group. You will often find that the wider the range of persons in the group —some your age, some older, some younger—the more enjoyment you will have.

WHEN TO GET MARRIED?

[14] There comes a time, however, when normally the young person wants to get married. When is the best time for this—when you still are in your teens? Generally not, for the hard facts show that most teen-age marriages simply do not have the same success as marriages where one or both

14. 15. (a) What do you think about the advisability of teen-age marriage? (b) What responsibility do parents have in connection with the desire of their children to marry?

persons have attained a more mature age. As one sociologist commented: "Research studies show that, in general, teen-age marriages are characterized by a high divorce or unhappiness rate compared with marriages at later age."

[15] On the other hand, there is no Scriptural basis for rigidly ruling out all marriage among such younger persons. Generally, the laws of the land grant the parents the right to exercise their mature judgment to decide what they believe will be in the best interests of their children and lead to the greatest happiness and benefit for them. They may decide either to allow or not to allow marriage of their sons or daughters who are under their jurisdiction. Certainly, the many problems of our times and the large percentage of marriage failures should cause them to exercise caution. And it should cause thinking young persons likewise to exercise caution—rather than to 'marry in haste and repent at leisure.' It is foolish to rush through a door just because it is open, when you do not have any good idea of what is on the other side.

CHOOSING A MARRIAGE MATE

[16] In some places a young man is allowed to be with a young girl only when at least one of the parents, or some other older person, is present. In many Western lands, however, such young persons may often be together without a chaperon. The question is, then, where such wider area of freedom is permitted, what can a young person

---

16-19. (a) In places where courtship is permitted, how will application of the principle at Galatians 5:13 prove beneficial? (b) What should be the goal of courtship? So what should those who engage in it be ready for? (c) Why is it to your advantage to get acquainted with a person of the opposite sex as part of a group, instead of off by yourselves?

do to assure that courtship will lead to a truly happy and successful marriage?

[17] Freedom always brings with it responsibility. So, if this question is one that you now face, you do well to keep in mind the fine principle set out in the Bible at Galatians 5:13. Here the apostle Paul was, of course, speaking of the spiritual freedom that Christianity brought to those embracing it. But the principle applies to any kind of freedom, especially if we want our exercise of it to bring fine results and God's favor. The apostle writes: "You were, of course, called for freedom, brothers; only do not use this freedom as an inducement for the flesh, but through love slave for one another." Genuine love—for God and for our neighbor, including the person we may be courting—will help us to avoid using any freedom we have in a selfish, harmful way.

[18] Properly, courting should be carried on with marriage as its goal. So, it should not begin before the person is ready to take on marriage responsibilities. Of course, you cannot know right at the start whether you want to marry a person or not. So it makes sense not to be too quick in settling your attention on any one individual. But this is no reason for carrying on "courtships" that amount to no more than a mere flirtation or a series of flirtations.

[19] Even if you are "interested" in someone, you would be wise, for a while, to try to keep your association with such one as merely part of a group, in group activities. Why? Because, in those circumstances, you can often get a better idea of what a person is really like. This is because

we all incline to be more "ourselves" when we are not under the pressure of feeling that someone is paying us special attention. But when a couple separates from the group, the natural tendency from then on is to be what the other person wants you to be, even to mirror his or her likes and dislikes. And sometimes this can camouflage one's real personality. When paired off, a couple can also quickly become emotionally involved so that they begin to see each other through "rose-colored glasses." If a couple get married under the flush of such emotion, they often face a rude awakening.

[20] Generally, it is the man who initiates courtship, by expressing interest in the woman. If he is honest and serious about it, she has the right to believe that he is at least contemplating marriage. Then what? Well, she then has a responsibility to ask herself whether she believes she could consider marriage with him. If she is quite certain that she would not consider him as a prospective husband, then it would be cruel for her to allow him to develop a deep interest in her. Some girls have been willing to let someone court them just to enhance their appearance of popularity or eligibility, hoping that other young men would now notice them. Some young men have done similarly, thinking they can "play the field," have a good time and then depart before things get too serious. But such selfish use of one's freedom can cause real hurt, severe wounds that may take months, even years, to heal.

20-22. (a) Why is an honest, unselfish approach to courtship important? (b) What can you learn about a prospective mate during courtship? What qualities would you particularly want in a mate?

[21] Only if used unselfishly can the freedom to court bring benefits. It can afford an opportunity to become better acquainted with the person with whom you are considering spending the rest of your life. Depending on how honest each one is toward the other, you can get to learn each other's likes and dislikes, standards, habits and outlooks, yes, and each other's temper and disposition and reaction to problems or difficulties. You rightly want to know such things as: Is he or she kind, generous and considerate of others? What about respect for parents and older persons? Is there good evidence of modesty and humility, or is the person boastful, stubborn? Do I see self-control and balance or, instead, weakness and childishness, perhaps sulking or even tantrums? Since a large part of life is work, what about signs of laziness, irresponsibility or a wasteful attitude toward money? What about plans for the future? Is a family desired or is there interest in some special vocation? In an article entitled "Danger Signals in Courtship," one writer states: "Our study of engaged and happily and unhappily married people found the unhappily married were in little agreement on life goals and values."

[22] Above all, you should want to know how much God's purposes figure in the other's interests and plans. Yes, when the whole picture is filled out, how well suited are you for each other? If serious differences exist, do not fool yourself into thinking that marriage will automatically solve them. It may only make the friction that they cause be felt more keenly.

HONORABLE CONDUCT IN COURTSHIP

[23] In lands where unchaperoned association is allowed by parents, couples who are courting often engage in expressions of affection such as holding hands, kissing, even embracing. Parents, of course, have the obligation to instruct their sons and daughters as to the standards by which they want them to conduct themselves. Elders in the Christian congregation can direct young people's attention to the sound guiding principles found in God's Word, and anyone who honestly wants to take a wise course in life will willingly and gladly give heed to such counsel.

[24] Not only does the Bible definitely rule out fornication, which is sexual intercourse by unmarried persons, including engaged couples, it also warns against immorality and "uncleanness," which can take place during courtship. (Galatians 5:19-21) Any couple that heed these warnings will save themselves much grief and will not run the risk of having the memories of some misconduct come back to trouble them. But what is unclean conduct according to the Bible's standards? What can it include?

[25] Holding hands can be a clean expression of affection between persons contemplating marriage. True, it does have a stimulating effect, but this is natural and not necessarily bad. Why, just the sight of the person one is considering marrying may also stimulate, 'making the heart beat faster.' (Song of Solomon 4:9) Nevertheless, we need to remember that, human nature being what it is, physical contact does increase the

---

23-26. (a) How do you feel about holding hands, kissing and embracing on the part of a couple that plan to get married? (b) How might one become guilty of "loose conduct" and "uncleanness"? Why is it important to avoid such things? (Galatians 5:19, 21)

"pull" of sexual attraction. So, because of realizing the possible consequences to which it might lead, some persons may prefer to limit themselves very strictly as to physical contact during courtship. And no one should disparage or make light of their conscientious position.

[26] Kissing may also be a clean expression of affection between persons contemplating marriage—or it may not be. Really, the question is, To what extent does passion enter the picture? Kissing can be done in a way that stirs passion to the point that a couple are deeply aroused sexually. Sexual arousal prepares the couple for intercourse, but this privilege, according to God's law, is reserved only for married persons. If a couple knowingly flaunt God's law by deliberately and brazenly engaging in passion-arousing conduct, whether by caressing each other's sexual

If courtship is a series of passionate expressions with less and less restraint, how will this affect prospects for a successful marriage?

organs or otherwise, they are guilty of "uncleanness" and "loose conduct."

[27] We ought to be honest with ourselves. If we know we do not have strong self-control in these things, then we should not jeopardize our future or that of the other person by taking chances. Would you drive a car down a steep winding road if you knew its brakes were in poor shape? The time to make up your mind and settle your heart on these matters is before you begin, not after. Once the physical desires begin to stir, it is generally very difficult to stop their buildup. Those who let passion build up in them to the point of desiring sexual relations—when they are not entitled to these through marriage—subject themselves to tension and frustration. It is like reading an exciting book—only to find that the last chapter has been torn out.

[28] Those who keep their relationship in courtship on a high level will get off to a far better start in marriage than those giving in to intimacy that steadily increases in frequency and intensity. How much respect can a girl feel for someone that she has to 'keep fighting off'? But a young man who shows respectful restraint and strength of willpower earns respect. The same is true of a girl. And she particularly needs to realize that, whereas her feelings may require time to be stirred, this is seldom true of a male. He can easily and quickly become sexually aroused.

[29] Giving in to frequent and increasingly pas-

27-30. What good reasons are there for avoiding passion-arousing conduct before marriage?

sionate expressions can lead to a premature marriage. The book *Adolescence and Youth* says: "The early stages of courtship are often impossibly romantic. Marriage at that time might lead a person to expect more of the marriage than any marriage could realize. Lengthened courtship usually brings about a more reasonable understanding of the other person so that an understanding marriage may result." For such longer courtship, restraint must be exercised—otherwise the power of sexual drive may build up so early as to become a real danger.

[30] Serious doubts and suspicions may also crop up after marriage if passion is allowed to color the picture strongly during the courtship period. The couple may begin to wonder, Did we really marry for love? Or were we just caught up in passion? Was it a wise choice? The girl may also incline to doubt the genuineness of her

There is much clean enjoyment that young people can share

husband's love, wondering if he did not marry her just for her body and not for what she is as a person.

[31] So, to protect yourself and your future happiness, avoid situations that lend themselves to passion. Lonely places and darkness are not going to help you to keep courtship honorable. Nor will situations where time hangs heavily and there seems to be nothing else to do except engage in such expressions of affection. But much clean enjoyment can be had in such activities as skating, playing tennis or similar sports, having a meal together at a restaurant or visiting some museum or local place of interest and beauty. While enjoying some feeling of privacy because of not being around personal acquaintances, you will have the safeguard of not being completely isolated from other people.

[32] Too, instead of thinking just about what you are "missing" by showing restraint, think about what you are preparing for in the future. Then, in all the years to come, you will be able to look back on your courtship, not with distaste or regret, but with pleasure and satisfaction.

31, 32. What can help a couple to avoid passion-arousing conduct that would mar their courtship?

Can You Succeed in Marriage?

I F THE time comes when you want to get married, it is natural that you should want your marriage to be successful. Judging from the sky-rocketing divorce rate, it might seem your prospects aren't very good. In some places the number of divorces are approaching the number of marriages! If you marry, how can you prevent problems from wrecking your marital happiness?

[2] Consideration of the origin of marriage will shed much light for you upon both the problems and the solution. Many believe that marriage is of human origin, that in some way it was worked out in the distant past by men. But this idea is at the very root of today's disastrous family breakdown. Why? Because it shoves aside as unimportant the very finest counsel on marital problems.

[3] Marriage is really of a higher origin. Almighty God himself created the first man and woman, gave them powers of reproduction and joined them together in marriage. God also provided instructions—recorded in the Bible—on how to make a success of marriage. Following these instructions closely is what will bring you happiness when you get married.

1-4. (a) Why is there good reason to be seriously concerned about one's prospects for a successful marriage? (b) To succeed in marriage, what must be recognized about its origin? Why? (Genesis 2:21-24; Matthew 19:4-6)

⁴ Some persons may object, saying that people have long had the Bible and yet their marriages have been failures. The increased divorce rate, they say, is because fewer couples are willing to put up with unhappy marriages. There is some truth in this argument. Millions of unhappy couples do *possess* the Bible. But have they *read* it? More importantly, have they *applied its principles* in their lives? The simple fact is, the Bible's advice has already helped hundreds of thousands of couples to handle their family problems successfully. If you want a happy marriage, it can help you too.

ENJOYABLE SEX IN MARRIAGE

⁵ You have probably heard it said that sex is at the root of many marriage problems, and this is true. This is often due to unrealistic views sponsored by the news media. Popular books, magazines and movies depict couples who "fall in love" and live "happily ever after." Literature also highlights sexual pleasures, often raising expectations beyond what realization fulfills. To illustrate, one young wife explained: "I guess I wanted sex to be some psychedelic jackpot that made the whole world light up like a pinball machine. I mean, it was all *right* but I kept thinking, 'Is that all there is? Is that all there *really* is?' "

⁶ Though, as a youth, you likely are not married, do you see the problem of this young wife? Her overriding concern was her *own* sexual enjoy-

---

5-10. (a) What unrealistic view as to sexual pleasure do many people have? (b) How can the applying of Bible counsel about unselfish giving help a couple to find contentment in this aspect of married life?

ment, and she was not satisfied. This is the complaint of many women—that their husbands don't satisfy them sexually. In such case, what can a wife do? Does the Bible say anything helpful? Note the straightforward encouragement it provides: "Let the husband render to his wife her due; but let the wife also do likewise to her husband. Do not be depriving each other of it, except by mutual consent."—1 Corinthians 7:3, 5.

⁷ According to this Bible counsel, if you get married, you should be concerned primarily with pleasing whom? Should it be your own self, as was the primary interest of the above-mentioned wife? No, but, rather, your mate. The underlying principle here in the Bible is of *giving*. The welfare and pleasure of your marriage mate, not yourself, is properly paramount. This is in harmony with the further Bible principles: "Let each one keep seeking, not his own advantage, but that of the other person." "Love . . . does not look for its own interests."—1 Corinthians 10:24; 13:4, 5.

⁸ But you may ask: "When I get married, how can seeking to please my wife or my husband increase *my* satisfaction?" Well, enjoyment of marital intercourse is largely dependent upon the mind and heart. Thus, if you view sexual relations as an opportunity to display deep love for your husband, you will more frequently, as a side result, find that you will enjoy the relations to a higher degree. When a wife's mind is not principally on her own sensations, she often relaxes, and the personal pleasure she really desires in the marriage act can be realized as a natural consequence.

⁹ The greatest teacher to walk the earth, Jesus Christ, indicated that giving of oneself will, in turn, bring a person satisfaction. He said: "There is more happiness in giving than there is in receiving." This principle has time and again proved true in connection with intimate marriage relations.—Acts 20:35.

¹⁰ There is another reason why applying Bible counsel is likely to work toward your own satisfaction when you get married. It will do more than anything else to move your husband to act unselfishly toward you, being more considerate of your needs and desires. It has happened this way in many marriages. The one taking the initiative in giving receives back in kind. Thus the Bible urges the showing of unselfishness and love in paying the marriage dues. Remember this, and it will contribute to a happy relationship if you get married.

¹¹ Perhaps you have heard that husbands frequently complain that their wives are too "cold" to be adequate sex partners. Do you know where the trouble often lies? The Bible states: "Husbands ought to be loving their wives as their own bodies. He who loves his wife loves himself, for no man ever hated his own flesh; but he feeds and cherishes it." (Ephesians 5:28, 29) Yes, the trouble often lies in the husband's failure to heed what the Bible here says.

¹² Do women really need to be loved by their husbands? Indeed they do. Marriage counselors often emphasize this. It is a basic truth: *For wives to be genuinely happy they need to feel that*

11-15. (a) What does a prospective husband need to realize about a wife's need for loving attention? (b) What does the Bible say as to the husband's responsibility in this regard?

they are loved. So if you should marry, remember that the key to warm marital intimacy is for you to fill this need of your wife to be loved. The Bible urges husbands: "Let each one of you individually so love his wife as he does himself." —Ephesians 5:33.

[13] However, it may be that you will feel that supporting your wife materially will be evidence enough of your love. But if expressions of affection are withheld, what will be the effect on her? The following letter from a wife may give you some idea. She wrote: "Here is my problem: I am so hungry . . . for a little sweet talk, a compliment,

**For a wife to be happy
she needs to feel she is loved**

the feel of his arm around my waist while I'm cooking—or a chance to sit in his lap. I'd trade all the material things I have for one affectionate squeeze."

[14] Yes, wives need to be *shown* love. They blossom out when they receive it, becoming more contented and often even more physically attractive. They were created with this need for love. That is why God urges husbands to love their wives. Failure to heed this counsel is a principal cause of the unhappiness found in so many marriages today. Why so?

[15] Because a wife starved for her husband's tenderness and affection is likely to feel insecure and lack confidence regarding her femininity. Even resentment toward her husband may develop, including perhaps a subconscious desire to get even with him for his neglect of her.

[16] You may feel, however, that it would be unmanly to treat with love and tenderness the woman you marry. You may even have heard it said that women really like it when they are treated in a rough way. But this is not true. In fact, sex relations for a wife may be unsatisfying, and even unpleasant, if her husband fails to appreciate that she was designed by God to respond to a kind, considerate man, not a harsh, demanding one.

[17] The Creator realized that husbands, confronted as they are with so many erroneous ideas, need instruction on how to love their wives. That is why he encourages them to be tender and considerate, saying: "You husbands, continue

---

16-18. (a) What misconception do some men have about how women like to be treated? (b) What is the meaning of the counsel at 1 Peter 3:7?

dwelling in like manner with [your wives] *according to knowledge, assigning them honor* as to a weaker vessel, the feminine one."—1 Peter 3:7.

[18] When it comes to sexual relations, it is especially important that a husband heed this instruction. He should act in accord with knowledge of how God made women. They usually are not as strong physically as men, and emotionally they are generally more delicate and sentimental than men. So God tells husbands to give wives honor as to a weaker vessel, to be respectful of their emotional makeup, limitations and vicissitudes.

SOLVING OTHER PROBLEMS

[19] Actually, sex is only a small part of marriage in which God's instructions need to be applied. When you get married, you will need to realize that your wife's biological cycle may, at times, affect her adversely in physical, mental and emotional ways. She may then do and say things that she would not ordinarily. You will need to take this into consideration, and not be overly sensitive if occasionally she speaks sharply or acts rashly, but continue to treat her with kindness.

[20] Yet much more is involved. Successful marriage requires cooperation and communication, and to achieve this an understanding of God's Word will help you. It shows that man and woman were created with somewhat different qualities

---

19. What else about a woman's makeup must a man take into account if they are to be happy together? (Colossians 3:12-14) 20-24. (a) God created woman with qualities that equip her for what role in marriage? (b) How can a wife show that she really does respect her husband's headship? (c) What is required of the husband in order to be a truly loving family head?

Really paying attention when your mate speaks is vital to a happy marriage

and responsibilities, with the purpose that their union contribute to mutual happiness. After creating man, the Creator said: "I am going to make a *helper* for him, as a *complement* of him."—Genesis 2:18.

²¹ The two were thus created to go together; their qualities balanced or complemented one another. Each was created with a need that the other filled. Thus woman was made as a helper to her husband, and in keeping with that role the Bible urges: "Let wives be in subjection to their husbands . . . because a husband is head of his wife." The Bible also says: "The wife should have deep respect for her husband." (Ephesians 5:22, 23, 33) This is practical, for if there is no head in the family who receives the respect of his wife, there are usually discord and confusion.

²² Today female aggressiveness and competition with men have become common, and these qualities are noted by marriage counselors to be a source of family problems. So when you get mar-

ried, you will be wise if you apply Bible counsel. If your husband fails to take the lead as he should, you will want to ask yourself: Can I do more to encourage him to fill his proper role in the family? Do I *ask* for his suggestions and guidance? Do I indicate that I am looking to him for leadership? Do I avoid belittling what he does? When in small ways he manifests willingness to make decisions or to take the lead in family affairs, do I express appreciation for this?

[23] But the man, in particular, is in position to make the marriage succeed by applying Bible counsel. Keep that in mind if you get married. Although you will then, as the husband, be head of the family, that does not make you a dictator. No, for God's Word commands husbands to love their wives, "just as the Christ also loved the [Christian] congregation and delivered up himself for it." (Ephesians 5:25) So, applying Bible counsel, you will lovingly and willingly make sacrifices for the woman you marry. Before making decisions you will do well to consider her opinions, her likes and dislikes, even giving her preference when there is no issue at stake. In this way you will show her *love* and *honor,* as the Bible commands.

[24] By thus heeding God's counsel, you will enjoy peace and harmony in your marriage, whenever the time for that may come. It will be a real success, resulting in the fulfillment and satisfaction that our Creator purposed for this grand arrangement to bring to humankind.

CHAPTER 21

How Do You View Material Possessions?

CAN you imagine a house literally full of thousands of fine gifts of all kinds and varieties? Would you like to live there and receive many of these gifts from your father as head of that home? Actually, you already live in such a home —this planet Earth—and Jehovah God has filled it with an amazing variety of good things.

² But, strangely enough, our getting full enjoyment from these material provisions—in fact, our getting full enjoyment from life itself—depends very much on our *not* making them the big thing in our lives. How can that be? It is because there are other things that are so much more valuable than material possessions.

³ You doubtless know some young people who give a lot of importance to material possessions. For some, what they seem to prize most is having a fancy radio or tape recorder, a stereo outfit, certain special items of clothing, a camera, a motor scooter or even their own car. Many persons show far more interest in those things than they do in their schooling, their families or anything else. They may also tend to evaluate you and others by what you have in the way of such material possessions. Does this make sense?

1-4. (a) What are some of the material possessions that many young folks like to have? (b) How can putting too much emphasis on material things cause one to have a distorted view of people?

⁴ Stop and think about it. Does your having or not having such material possessions really make any difference in what you are as a person? Are you a better person if you have them, or a worse person if you don't? Actually, the most valuable possessions, the ones that really determine your worth as a person and the ones that can bring you the most satisfaction and happiness, are of

a different kind. Can you think of what some of these more valuable possessions would be?

MORE VALUABLE POSSESSIONS

⁵ What about *knowledge?* Compare the value, say, of knowing another language with owning a stereo outfit or a transistor radio. True, there is nothing wrong with having those items, and you can enjoy hearing other people talk and sing—in your language. But with knowledge of a second language you yourself might be able to talk with as many as one hundred million more people on earth than you can with just the language you

5-7. (a) How can knowledge of a second language, or of how to do things, be more valuable than material possessions? (Ecclesiastes 7:12) (b) Why is knowledge of God's Word even more valuable? (Proverbs 15:2; 1 Timothy 4:16)

presently know. Persons using that language may visit where you live. Or, if you ever have opportunity to travel to other lands, such knowledge could add immensely to your enjoyment of the trip.

[6] Similarly with getting knowledge of *how to do things*. Think of how valuable it is to learn how to be a good cook, a capable seamstress, a skilled carpenter, or to be good at making mechanical repairs. These abilities could be of far greater future value to you in doing something worth while in your life than just having certain material possessions.

[7] The most valuable knowledge is that of God's Word. Why is that true? Because with it you can bring comfort and hope to persons who are heartbroken and in despair, yes, in a way that music from a stereo set never could. You can, in fact, even save lives with knowledge of God's truth. What material possession can you think of that would do that? No wonder the wise man urges young persons to make the purchase he recommends when saying: "Buy truth itself and do not sell it—wisdom and discipline and understanding. The father of a righteous one will without fail be joyful; the one becoming father to a wise one will also rejoice in him. Your father and your mother will rejoice, and she that gave birth to you will be joyful."—Proverbs 23:23-25.

[8] Think, too, how much more valuable a good name or reputation is than having material possessions. If you are known for being unselfish, honest, diligent, reliable and respectful, that can

---

8-12. (a) Why is it that what you are as a person is of greater value than what you possess materially? How does the Bible show this? (b) So, what qualities should we endeavor to cultivate? (Galatians 5:22, 23)

make you a welcome sight far more than any special kind of clothes could ever do. Such a reputation can cause you to be sought after as a valuable friend or as a workmate or employee. It can bring invitations from persons to visit them or to do things with them, to share their good things with them. Wouldn't this solve any problem of loneliness far better than even a television set?

⁹ Really, so much of our happiness in life depends on our having the assurance that we are appreciated, that we matter to others, that we contribute something to their lives that they would miss if we were not living. Being rich in fine qualities will cause you to be appreciated far more by the best of people than would your being rich in material possessions. As the book of wise sayings puts it: "The one loving purity of heart—for the charm of his lips the king will be his companion."—Proverbs 22:11.

¹⁰ The young man Timothy had the privilege of being selected to accompany the apostle Paul on his missionary journeys to many interesting places. This was not because of Timothy's material possessions but because of his fine qualities, reported on by Christians in two cities of Asia Minor. The experience that Timothy gained as a result was beyond price. It qualified him later to take on special assignments, and to be the type of man in whom the apostle could place great trust. That Timothy did not make material possessions the big thing in his life is seen from Paul's statement made when sending Timothy to the congregation in Philippi in Macedonia: "I have no one else of a disposition like his who will genuinely care for the things pertaining to you.

For all the others are seeking their own interests, not those of Christ Jesus. But you know the proof he [Timothy] gave of himself."—Philippians 2:19-23.

¹¹ True friends will appreciate you for what you *are* and not for what you have. "A friend is a loving companion at all times, and a brother is born to share troubles." (Proverbs 17:17, *New English Bible*) More than this, Jehovah himself will be your friend if you make his service the big thing in your life, and "when Jehovah takes pleasure in the ways of a man he causes even his enemies themselves to be at peace with him." —Proverbs 16:7.

¹² Realize, too, that such things as knowledge, a fine personality and genuine friends are not things that can be stolen nor do they wear out and lose their value with time and use. But people can steal or destroy your material possessions. God's Son wisely counseled therefore: "Store up for yourselves treasures in heaven, where neither moth nor rust consumes, and where thieves do not break in and steal. For where your treasure is, there your heart will be also." (Matthew 6:20, 21) If you have and maintain a good name with God, your future happiness is secure, certain. In his new order you will be able to enjoy to the full all the treasure of good things that this earth contains.

SHOW STRENGTH AND WISDOM

¹³ So, then, why let the present commercial systems with their high-powered advertising

---

13-15. (a) If the desire for material possessions controlled your life, whom would you enrich? But how would you lose out? (Matthew 6:33) (b) What view of material possessions is a balanced one?

pressure you into building your life around material possessions? Why enrich them and in the end make yourself poor as far as the really worthwhile things in life are concerned? Why not show real strength to resist the pull of materialism and be determined to get the most out of life by seeking things of greater value than material possessions?

[14] This is especially vital now. Bible prophecies show that the present system, with all its commercialism, is nearing its end. Making too much of material things would be a trap for us, diverting our attention. We could find ourselves bogged down in this system and be swept away with it when God cleans it out and brings in his new order. As Jesus warned: "Keep your eyes open and guard against every sort of covetousness, because even when a person has an abundance his life does not result from the things he possesses." —Luke 12:15.

[15] Not that we should be without any possessions at all. But we don't want them to control our life. And we should be able to distinguish between possessions that will really contribute to genuine happiness and those that actually could hinder us in gaining our goal. Whatever possessions you have, then, make it your aim to use them for the good of others and especially to honor your Creator.

CHAPTER 22

Honesty—Does It Pay?

MOST people today don't think it makes sense to tell the truth all the time. Have you observed that? Many businessmen claim they could not compete successfully without some dishonesty. Advertisements come into our view daily that exaggerate or misrepresent. Though political leaders are supposed to be watching over the public's welfare, many people view them as untrustworthy.

² Seeing so much dishonesty among adults, young people often adopt the same course. Many cheat on tests in school or "cut classes" under false pretenses. To their friends they may brag, painting false pictures of what they are or what they have done. At home, they may even deceive their parents—answering questions about their conduct with half-truths, hiding the facts by phrasing their answers so as to give entirely false impressions. If their parents or others try to find out how they feel about immorality, drugs or similar things, they may smoothly cover over the facts, saying what they think those questioning them *want* to hear, not how they really feel. To get money or permission to do something, they may shower a parent with insincere affection or with flattery.

³ But is this really strange? The fact is, many

_____

1-4. Among younger folks, what evidences of dishonesty have you observed? Why isn't it really surprising that many young folks do these things? (Isaiah 9:16)

young people feel they are justified in doing this. Why? Well, it's true that their parents may teach them that it is wrong to lie. Yet they may see their parents misrepresent facts in order to get out of some unpleasant situation or to avoid paying some bill, debt or tax. Have you noticed that some parents even use their children to falsify for them in giving excuses?

4 Where conditions like these prevail, what encouragement is there for young people—or for any of us—to strive to be honest in all things? In a world where lying, cheating and stealing are so common, how practical and worth while is it for you to hold to what is true? Will it really bring you greater benefit than dishonesty would, and, if so, what kind of benefit?

SHORT-TERM VERSUS LONG-TERM BENEFITS

5 Ask yourself: What do I want—a quick gain, an apparent benefit, or that which brings enduring benefits? When you think about it, isn't it true that any apparent benefits from lying and cheating are short term at best? Yes, God's Word is really true when it says: "It is the lip of truth that will be firmly established forever, but the tongue of falsehood will be only as long as a moment."—Proverbs 12:19.

6 Take, as an example, a businessman who misrepresents some product. He may make a sale, but in the process he may lose a customer when the person finds out he was cheated. Or, suppose you were to cheat in school. If not caught, you might get higher grades. But what good would even "straight A's" be if you got out of school

5-7. Why are any benefits of dishonesty only temporary?

with very little knowledge, maybe not even being able to read or add well?

[7] In the end, then, the person who cheats actually cheats himself most of all. Just compare the honest and the dishonest person. And consider some of the things the dishonest person stands to lose and see if you don't agree that anyone who thinks that dishonesty helps toward a better or happier life is really very shortsighted.

[8] If you are known for being straightforward and honest in your dealings, you earn the respect and trust of others. The friends you gain are more likely to be genuine because they find you genuine and appreciate this. While it is true that the modern business world is often dishonest, it is also true that employers generally have enough sense to value employees who are honest. A reputation for honesty, then, can bring employment when employment is scarce or aid in holding on to a job when others are losing theirs.

Do you really benefit if you steal?

8-10. How is honesty beneficial (a) in one's secular work? (b) in family relationships? (c) in connection with friends?

⁹ At home, honesty contributes to a comfortable, pleasant atmosphere, eliminating doubts or suspicions between marriage partners and between parents and children. When by their honesty children win their parents' full confidence, usually the parents are willing gradually to grant youngsters more freedom. Granted, telling the truth about some mistake or wrong act can bring discipline. But that discipline may well be lighter because you were honest. Then, if, in the future, you truthfully deny having done some wrong, your explanation is more likely to be believed.

¹⁰ Contrast this with the person who gives in to dishonesty to "get out of a pinch" or to gain some advantage. He risks losing all these fine benefits. Because dealing with a dishonest person is like riding in a car with a steering defect—you never know just what he may do. So realize that when you lie to someone or cheat him, the distrust you create may take years to erase. Where a parent or a friend is involved, the wound caused may heal but may leave a bad memory that is like a long-lasting scar. If you make a practice of dishonesty, the time may well come when you seriously want and need others to believe and trust you but they cannot. Is any temporary advantage that dishonesty brings worth this?

¹¹ Actually, lying is like wading into quicksand. Often each lie calls for other lies to back it up, and one is soon enmeshed in a vicious cycle. Surely, can't we see the wisdom of the straightforward Bible counsel: "Do not be lying to one another"?—Colossians 3:9.

¹² Those who lie often begin with half-truths

11-13. (a) How does the habit of lying often get started? (b) Why is it cowardly, rather than courageous, to lie?

and "little lies," then gradually go on to worse ones. Lying thus often gets started as does gambling. The person gambling begins betting small amounts, but—usually to cover some losses—he gradually gets drawn into making bigger and bigger bets.

[13] At first, telling falsehoods with a straight face may seem bold, daring. You may even know of persons who train themselves to look another straight in the eye while lying. Is that not courageous? No, lying is actually cowardly rather than courageous. What takes courage is to tell the truth and face up to whatever consequences that brings. Rather than implying strength, a lie is weak, unable to stand on its own, needing other lies to hold it up, never willing to meet the truth face to face. Why, then, be like a person who spends his life wearing a false face, hiding, ducking and making excuses? Why be like Judas Iscariot, who became a cheat, tried to lead a double life and wound up a failure and a suicide? Why not be man or woman enough to be honest? It is the only way to maintain self-respect and a good conscience.

KEEPING YOUR WORD

[14] Keeping your word is also involved in this matter of honesty. You would probably feel deeply hurt if your parents promised you something and then failed to fulfill their word. But do you feel as strongly about keeping your word to your parents? What are you like in this respect? If you tell someone you will help him to do something or offer to perform some service, do you try always to fulfill your word? If you make

---

14-16. Why is it important to keep your word?

an appointment to meet someone at a certain time, do you show up, and on time? How much is your word worth?

15 Youth is the right time to start developing the habit of being a person of your word. Keeping or not keeping your word tells a lot about what you are like inside now; it also has a molding effect on your mind and heart. It builds up an attitude, a way of looking at things that can produce long-lasting personality traits.

16 If you are reliable now, you probably will be in later years. And the reverse is just as true. For example, if you do not live up to your word now, in later years you may make a firm agreement to take on a certain job or assignment— and then soon want to back out. Many people do that, but they are not viewed with respect by others.

17 Why do people break their word? Well, for one thing keeping one's word puts limitations on a person, it obligates him. When the time arrives for keeping an appointment or some other promise, something else may seem more appealing. Then, too, many times the person may find that making good on his word means much harder work than he thought it would.

18 What will you do in such cases? Will you stay by your word even though it means some hardship or loss to you? One may say, "But I didn't know what I was getting into!" The real question here is: Whose fault was it? Was there fraud or deception on the other person's side? If not, then if you endure whatever hardness ful-

---

17-19. (a) Why do people break their word? (b) What can help you to avoid situations where you might feel inclined to break your word?

filling your word requires, you learn a valuable lesson. That is: *Think before you talk, before you give your word. Then, when you speak, mean what you say.*

¹⁹ To say "Yes" to something simply because you think it will please someone—but without first thinking out the consequences—can get you into difficulty. By contrast, if you are careful about making promises, if you think matters through and consider how they will affect your future life, then it will be much easier to keep your word once you have committed yourself. You will have prepared your heart and mind to be true to your word. "Let your word *Yes* mean Yes," Jesus said.—Matthew 5:37.

THE MAIN REASON WHY HONESTY PAYS

²⁰ The main reason why it pays to be honest and truthful is that Jehovah God counts as his friends only persons who are. Why so? Because he himself is unfailingly true to his word. That is why Joshua could say to the nation of Israel: "You well know with all your hearts and with all your souls that not one word out of all the good words that Jehovah your God has spoken to you has failed. They have all come true for you. Not one word of them has failed." (Joshua 23:14) The Bible is largely a record of the promises Jehovah has kept. His trueness in the past is what gives us such confidence of future blessings in fulfillment of his promises.

²¹ Do you want God's approval? Then remember that he gives it only to those who worship him

20-22. (a) What is the main reason why it is important to be honest at all times? (Psalm 15:1-4) (b) What fine example does God set in keeping his word? What can help us to follow His example?

"with spirit and truth." (John 4:23) And keep in mind that he detests lying in all its forms—deception, boasting, slander, cheating—because it springs from selfishness, greed and a callous unconcern for the interests of others. He knows that all mankind's troubles and suffering originally stem from lying—on the part of the "father of the lie," Satan, God's principal enemy.—John 8:44.

[22] Do you sincerely want to hold faithfully to a course of honesty? Then you should realize that only genuine love for your Creator and your neighbor can give you the motivation you need. There must be a heartfelt love of truth for the good it does and an equally intense hatred of lying for the harm it does. God's approval, too, must mean more to you than that of any other person. Remember, it is only because he himself loves the truth and hates lying that we can have a solid hope for the future, based on his unfailing promises and the proved reliability of his Word. So strive to be like him. Keep in mind that "it is the lip of truth that will be firmly established forever, but the tongue of falsehood will be only as long as a moment."—Proverbs 12:19.

CHAPTER 23

What Do You Want
out of Life?

IN YOUTH your life is largely ahead of you. It probably seems to stretch out for a long way, like a road with its end somewhere beyond the horizon. Where will it lead you?

[2] There is no doubt that the road of life will hold some surprises for you, along with some disappointments. But, as we have seen in this book, there is a lot you can do now to make sure that you get the best out of life. The question is, Are you willing to put forth the effort needed?

[3] Many young people think about what activity they will pursue when they finish school. Perhaps you too have thought about that. But no matter what kind of work you do, if you do it poorly it won't bring you much satisfaction. There is something far more important than this, though.

[4] Suppose you do become a very fine architect or artist, mechanic, musician, farmer, schoolteacher, or whatever it might be. Is this a sure guarantee that your life will be happy? Not really. Far more important is: What *kind of person* are you going to be? Many people have had a brilliant career in some profession but have made a miserable failure of their personal lives; they were very unhappy individuals.

1-6. (a) To get the best out of life, what must you be willing to do? (b) For you to have a happy life, what is even more important than excelling in a certain career? (c) Why can the Bible help you in this?

⁵ That is why the Bible is so important. Really, the whole Bible is somewhat like a collection of letters from our Creator. As our heavenly Father he is interested in our happiness, and we should be interested in what he has to tell us. We have seen the guidelines that he gives us in answer to so many of our problems. And isn't it true that it all makes sense? Really without those guidelines from him, how could we be sure of what to do, or know what would work out for the best?

⁶ This calls to mind what the apostle Paul wrote to a younger fellow worker, Timothy. Paul urged him to keep on in the things he had learned since childhood about the Bible's teachings and said: "All Scripture is inspired of God and beneficial for teaching, for reproving, for setting things straight, for disciplining in righteousness, that the man of God may be fully competent, completely equipped for every good work." (2 Timothy 3:14-17) Anything that is really worth while in life—no matter what kind of activity it may involve—you will be better equipped to do it and do it *well* if you let yourself be guided by God's Word. It can make you a better son or daughter, a better husband or wife, a better father or mother, a better worker, a better friend and, above all, a better servant of your Creator.

TAKING ON RESPONSIBILITY

⁷ Sooner or later you will have some serious decisions to make. The time will come when you will have to take on your own load of responsibility. Right now you are something like a young eagle. You may know that eagles often

7-11. As shown in the Bible, what is the key to getting the very best out of life?

build their nest high up on the edge of a towering cliff. When the young ones start fluttering their wings and are ready to fly, the parent eagles will edge them to the side of the nest and then—out into the air! One observer tells of watching a parent eagle letting the young one drop about ninety feet before swooping underneath and, with outspread wings, letting the young bird alight on its back. Then a soaring flight back up to the nest and the process was repeated until the young eagle had learned to fly.—*Bulletin of the Smithsonian Institution,* Vol. CLXVII, page 302.

⁸ In your case, your parents have built up a home with much effort and planning. But you cannot forever count on them to do things for you or to make big decisions for you. This would be especially true if, on coming of age, you should decide to leave home. Your parents can help to prepare you for taking on responsibility as a grown man or woman, making it easier for you until you are able to be on your own, just as the parent eagle does for its young. But you will have to do your part also.

⁹ The design of the eagle's powerful wings and its instinctive ability to fly—these things originally came from an all-wise Creator. So each of us needs to realize that the key to getting the best out of life is found in our reliance on Him. No matter how fine (or how poor) a start your parents may be able to give you, and no matter how good a mind and body you may have, you will always want to appreciate the need for guidance from Jehovah God and look to him for strength to follow his leadings. He inspired these words to be written for young persons like yourself:

[10] "To my sayings incline your ear. May they not get away from your eyes. Keep them in the midst of your heart. For they are life to those finding them and health to all their flesh. More than all else that is to be guarded, safeguard your heart, for out of it are the sources of life. . . . As for your eyes, straight ahead they should look, yes, your own beaming eyes should gaze straight in front of you. Smooth out the course of your foot, and may all your own ways be firmly established."—Proverbs 4:20-26.

[11] The more you look to Jehovah God and his Word for direction, the smoother the road of life will become for you.

HAVING GOD AS YOUR FRIEND

[12] How can you do this? It isn't simply by avoiding things that God's Word shows to be wrong. You need to have a *personal relationship* with Jehovah as your heavenly Father. Your parents may be able to point you in that direction, but they can't establish that relationship for you. You must do that yourself, seeking Jehovah's friendship. If you want the Maker of this vast universe as your friend, what does he require of you?

[13] To open the way for this, Jehovah God sent his firstborn Son on an assignment to this planet Earth, causing him to be born as a human. When he became a full-grown man, God's Son gave his life on our behalf. As the Bible says: "We behold Jesus, who has been made a little lower than angels, crowned with glory and honor for having suffered death, that he by God's undeserved kind-

---

12, 13. (a) Besides avoiding what the Bible says is wrong, what else do we need if God is to be our friend? (b) How was the way opened for us to have such a relationship? (John 14:6)

ness might taste death for every man."—Hebrews 2:9.

¹⁴ The Bible shows that the reason this was needed is that we are all imperfect and sinful. That shouldn't be hard for you to recognize as true, because at times you probably have found it a real struggle to keep from doing things that you knew were wrong. Very likely you have at times weakened and given in to some wrong desire. This inborn leaning toward wrongdoing is something that we all inherited from our first parents, and that is why the whole human race is in a dying condition.

¹⁵ But God's Son gave his perfect human life so as to provide the means for canceling out all our wrongdoing. The Bible helps us to understand how this works by likening sins to "debts." (Matthew 6:12) For example, if you spread around some false rumor about someone else, wouldn't you say that you "owed" him an apology? That means you are in "debt" to him because of the wrong you did. But the debt we have toward God is so big that we could never pay it ourselves. Christ Jesus' perfect human life, however, is of such great value that it can cancel out all the debts we incur against God due to inherited sinfulness, and that is why God's Son gave up his life on our behalf.

¹⁶ So the way is open for us to have friendship with God. But we have to show that we appreciate what he has done in sacrificing his own Son

14, 15. (a) What can all of us see in our lives that shows that we are imperfect? (Romans 5:12; 7:21-23) (b) At Matthew 6:12, to what are sins likened? How can that "debt" be paid? 16-18. (a) Why do you feel that God deserves our appreciation for what was done by means of his Son? (Romans 5:6-10) (b) What are some of the things that we can do to show that appreciation?

and what his Son did in dying for us. We have to show that we have faith in this provision of God. Jesus said: "The Father loves the Son and has given all things into his hand. He that exercises faith in the Son has everlasting life; he that disobeys the Son will not see life, but the wrath of God remains upon him."—John 3:35, 36.

[17] Just suppose you were to save a person's life —perhaps saving someone from drowning or from dying in a burning house—and as a result of doing this you yourself then died. What if the person who was saved didn't show any gratitude at all, didn't even bother to go to your parents and say something in appreciation for your unselfish act? How do you think your own father would feel? You can understand, then, why Jehovah God is rightly grieved and withholds his friendship from those who know about what his Son did for mankind but who show no appreciation for it.

[18] You can show appreciation by the life you live. You can show that you sincerely regret the wrongs you have committed and ask God to 'cover your debts' by means of his Son's sacrifice. You can dedicate yourself to God to serve him for the rest of your life, doing what pleases him. The Bible shows that we can symbolize this dedication by water baptism. Of course, this is not something to be done hastily. You can't say to God that you're going to do something and then change your mind. That's the way little children are; they aren't really sure what they want to do. But as you approach manhood or womanhood, you are reaching the point in life where you can decide. So it is something for you to be thinking seriously about.

FACING UP TO THE CHALLENGE

[19] To keep proving that you are God's friend will not always be easy. In fact, the Bible shows that you will have a big challenge because the world as a whole is not God's friend but his enemy. But do not lose heart. You can show the same spirit that God's servant David did when he was a young lad. He had come to the army camp of the Israelites at a time when they were confronted by the forces of the Philistines, who were worshipers of false gods. The Philistines' champion—a giant of a man named Goliath—was taunting the Israelites, daring them to do battle with him. David heard this. Though only a youth, he had strong faith in Jehovah. He took up the challenge, advanced on the hulking, heavily armed foe and dropped him with a single stone from his shepherd's sling.

[20] Today you face an enemy world, but have no fear. Jehovah is the same Almighty God that he was in David's day and you can gain a victory if you show courage and, above all, faith that He will never abandon you but will back you up and give you the needed strength.

[21] Some men and women, including many young persons, have endured hardships, risked their lives or even died in order to serve the interests of some political government of earth. What a far greater honor it is, however, to serve the interests of the Creator of the whole universe! Consider now how this can give you a life that is far, far better than the life that anyone on earth today enjoys.

19-21. (a) How is the challenge that you face similar to the one that faced David when he went out to fight Goliath? (1 Samuel 17:4-11, 26-51; John 15:17-20; James 4:4) (b) Why can we be confident that it is possible to meet this challenge successfully? (John 16:33; Philippians 4:13; Proverbs 3:5, 6)

CHAPTER 24

A Grand Future
in Store for You

IN MANY ways you live at a most favored time in human history. Not because of the way world conditions are today but because of what the Bible shows the near future is due to bring.

² Jehovah God knows how much there is need for a change—a big change—in things here on this planet. He is clearly the only One who can bring about that change. The world of mankind is now thousands of years old. But it is still wrestling with the same old problems that have continually troubled human society: war, hunger, poor housing, injustice, economic problems.

³ The things that need straightening out in the present world system are really too many to number. Surely there must be something better than this. And the Bible shows that Jehovah God does have something far better in store for those who love and serve him. In fact, he has been using some six thousand years to unfold his purpose for bringing about a completely new order, a paradise of pleasure. In that new and delightful order of things he promises to eliminate once and for all time the corrupt and violent and selfish conditions that rob life of so much of its joy.

1-3. (a) Why do we live at a most favored time in human history? (b) What change is God going to bring about for our benefit?

HOW AND WHEN CHANGE WILL COME

[4] How will he do this? First of all by doing away with the mixed-up and ineffective rule of this earth under the hundreds of political systems now operating. He declares his purpose to replace them with a single government of his own making, his kingdom by his Son Jesus Christ. God caused the prophet Daniel to foretell that, saying: "In the days of those kings [or rulerships] the God of heaven will set up a kingdom that will never be brought to ruin. And the kingdom . . . will crush and put an end to all these kingdoms, and it itself will stand to times indefinite." (Daniel 2:44) When will this happen? There is a way of knowing when it is near.

[5] If you live in a temperate zone of the earth and you see the leaves on the trees turn brown and fall off, and you see the skies daily becoming grayer and feel the air becoming crisp and cool, and you see flocks of birds flying toward a warmer zone of the earth—without looking at the calendar you know that winter is approaching, don't you? It is not just any one of those things that tells you that, because skies can become gray even on a summer day, or trees might become diseased and lose their leaves. But all those things put together make up a sure sign of winter's approach.

[6] In a similar way, there is a "sign" made up of many features that the Bible gives. And this sign tells us that the time is at hand for God's kingdom by Christ Jesus to take control of this earth. You can see that sign today just by looking at newspapers or through news programs on radio and television. What is it?

4-8. (a) How will Jehovah bring about the needed change? (b) What proves that the time for this to take place is very near? (2 Timothy 3:1-5; Matthew 24:7, 8, 32, 33)

⁷ Jesus foretold that within a certain generation there would come a time especially marked by wars, hunger, disease and earthquakes, along with much anxiety and uncertainty as to what the future would bring upon the earth. Aren't those the very things we are continuously faced with today through the news sources? No generation before in human history has seen all those things in such quantity as the generation living on the earth since 1914. This is why historians call 1914 a "turning point" in mankind's history.

⁸ Speaking of the generation seeing that "sign," Jesus said: "When you see these things occurring, know that the kingdom of God is near. Truly I say to you, This generation will by no means pass away until all things occur." (Luke 21:31, 32) This means that God's new order has drawn near. What changes will it bring?

CHANGES GOD HAS IN STORE FOR THE HUMAN FAMILY

⁹ By placing this planet and its inhabitants under the rule of just one perfect, heaven-directed government, God promises to stop for all time the political bickering and fighting that waste so much of the world's wealth. That will mean the end of wars that take the cream of the nations' youth and, afterward, send them back with large numbers crippled, having hands, arms or legs amputated, perhaps blind or, worse, in the form of lifeless corpses. Those who live in God's new order will all be peace-loving persons who have carried out the Bible prophecy at Isaiah 2:4: "They will have to beat their swords into plow-

9-13. (a) In God's new order, what conditions are going to exist for all mankind? (b) What convinces you that these things really can and will take place? (Revelation 21:5)

shares and their spears into pruning shears. Nation will not lift up sword against nation, neither will they learn war anymore." With peace prevailing earth wide, wonderful things can then be accomplished for the good of all people everywhere.

[10] Not only will political corruption and waste stop. The greed of giant commercial systems will also be brought to a halt. Many of these systems are dirtying up the earth, polluting the air, the water, the land, killing off earth's wildlife. But the Bible tells us, at Revelation 11:18, that God is going to "bring to ruin those ruining the earth." Then, the beauty of earth's forests, the sparkling clearness of its streams and lakes, the freshness and fragrance of its air, and the rich variety of its bird, fish and animal wildlife will all be restored. You can be among those enjoying these things in the grand future that God has in store for those putting faith in his Word.

[11] Our Creator promises that, in his new order, the rich produce of the earth will be enjoyed by all persons, wherever they may live. No more on this earth will you see starving children with bloated bellies and shriveled arms, as is true in many parts of the earth today. At Isaiah 25:6, 8, God caused this prophecy to be written: "And Jehovah of armies will certainly make for all the peoples . . . a banquet of well-oiled dishes . . . He will actually swallow up death forever, and the Sovereign Lord Jehovah will certainly wipe the tears from all faces."

[12] Yes, best of all, the Bible shows that God is going to restore perfect health to obedient mankind. All the sadness and suffering that disease and pain and death have brought will end

forever as his Son's kingdom brings the curing of human sickness and imperfection. Revelation 21:4 tells us: "He will wipe out every tear from their eyes, and death will be no more, neither will mourning nor outcry nor pain be anymore. The former things have passed away."

[13] That means the time will come when the process of aging that results from human imperfection will be eliminated. How loving of God to provide for a future that will be free from such things as wrinkles, graying hair or baldness, brittle bones, loss of muscle tone, shortness of breath and all the other things that now come with old age. Yes, and for persons already old, God is able to do what Job 33:25 describes, saying: "Let his flesh become fresher than in youth; let him return to the days of his youthful vigor." Yes, Jehovah God can bring health and strength that are actually better than what youth today has, because even young people now get sick and some die unexpectedly at an early age.

HOW YOU CAN ENJOY THE FUTURE

[14] That grand future can be yours if you do as the Bible says: "Remember, now, your Grand Creator in the days of your young manhood [or young womanhood], before the calamitous days proceed to come, or the years have arrived when you will say [as people suffering from old age say]: 'I have no delight in them.' "—Ecclesiastes 12:1.

[15] It is not just a matter of thinking of your Creator now and then. It is a matter of remembering him every day and all day long by seeking

14-16. What do you need to do in order to enjoy this grand future?

to live in a way that pleases him and that will make him want to have you among those who will live in his new order. He will not force you to do this. You must do it of your own choice and free will. You know that when your parents have to force you to do something that you should do, then they get no real pleasure out of seeing you do it. But if you do it willingly and gladly because you know it pleases them, you bring them much happiness. So, too, Jehovah in his Word says: "Be wise, my son, and make my heart rejoice."—Proverbs 27:11.

[16] Yes, enjoy your youth, the springtime of your life, and get the best out of it. Build the qualities that will bring you the greatest happiness possible, both now and in the future. Use your youth to get a fine start on the road to life, not just to a few short decades of life in this present dying, decaying system of things, but to eternal life in the freshness of youthful vigor on God's paradise earth. ◊◊◊◊◊◊◊◊◊◊◊◊◊◊◊◊◊◊◊◊◊◊◊◊◊

For further information write WATCH TOWER at an address given below

ALASKA 99507: 2552 East 48th Ave., Anchorage. AUSTRALIA: Box 280, Ingleburn, N.S.W. 2565; Zouch Road, Denham Court, N.S.W. 2565. BAHAMAS: Box N-1247, Nassau, N.P. BARBADOS: Fontabelle Rd., Bridgetown. BELIZE: Box 257, Belize City. BRAZIL: Rodovia SP-141, Km 43, 18280 Cesario Lange, SP; Caixa Postal 92, 18270 Tatuí, SP. CANADA L7G 4Y4: Box 4100, Halton Hills (Georgetown), Ontario. ENGLAND NW7 1RN: The Ridgeway, London. FIJI: Box 23, Suva. FRANCE: 81 rue du Point-du-Jour, F-92100 Boulogne-Billancourt. GERMANY, FEDERAL REPUBLIC OF: Postfach 20, D-6251 Selters/Taunus 1. GHANA: Box 760, Accra. GUAM 96913: 143 Jehovah St., Barrigada. GUYANA: 50 Brickdam, Georgetown 16. HAWAII 96819: 2055 Kam IV Rd., Honolulu. HONG KONG: 4 Kent Road, Kowloon Tong. INDIA: Post Bag 10, Lonavla, Pune Dis., Mah. 410 401. IRELAND: 29A Jamestown Road, Finglas, Dublin 11. JAMAICA: Box 180, Kingston 10. KENYA: Box 47788, Nairobi. LEEWARD ISLANDS: Box 119, St. Johns, Antigua. LIBERIA: P.O. Box 171, Monrovia. MALAYSIA: 28 Jalan Kampar, Off Jalan Landasan, 41300 Klang, Sel. NEW ZEALAND: P.O. Box 142; 198 Mahia Rd., Manurewa. NIGERIA: PMB 001, Shomolu, Lagos State. PAKISTAN: 197-A Ahmad Block, New Garden Town, Lahore 16. PANAMA: Apartado 1835, Panama 9A. PAPUA NEW GUINEA: Box 636, Boroko, N.C.D. PHILIPPINES, REPUBLIC OF: P.O. Box 2044, 1099 Manila; 186 Roosevelt Ave., San Francisco del Monte, 1105 Quezon City. PORTUGAL: Rua Conde Barão, 511, Alcabideche, P-2765 Estoril; Apartado 91, P-2766 Estoril Codex. SIERRA LEONE: P. O. Box 136, Freetown. SOUTH AFRICA: Private Bag 2067, Krugersdorp, 1740. SRI LANKA, REP. OF: 62 Layard's Road, Colombo 5. SWITZERLAND: Ulmenweg 45; P.O. Box 225, CH-3602 Thun. TRINIDAD AND TOBAGO, REP. OF: Lower Rapsey Street & Laxmi Lane, Curepe. UNITED STATES OF AMERICA: 25 Columbia Heights, Brooklyn, N.Y. 11201. ZIMBABWE: 35 Fife Avenue, Harare.